3 CRUCIAL
QUESTIONS
ABOUT JESUS

3 Crucial Questions
Grant R. Osborne and *Richard J. Jones, Jr.*, editors

3 CRUCIAL QUESTIONS ABOUT JESUS

Murray J. Harris

Baker Books

A Division of Baker Book House Co
Grand Rapids, Michigan 49516

To My Brothers
Bruce, Evan, Donald, Robin

Published by Baker Books, a division of Baker Book House Company
P.O. Box 6287, Grand Rapids, Michigan 49516-6287

Second printing, December 1995

Printed in the United States of America

Library of Congress Cataloging-in-Publication Data

Harris, Murray J.
   3 crucial questions about Jesus / Murray J. Harris.
     p.   cm.
   Includes bibliographical references and index.
   ISBN 0-8010-4388-3
    1. Jesus Christ—Historicity. 2. Jesus Christ—Divinity. 3. Jesus Christ—
Resurrection. I. Title. II. Title: Three crucial questions about Jesus.
BT202.H295   1994
232.9'08—dc20
                                               93-46097

Contents

Editors' Preface

The books in the 3 Crucial Questions series are the published form of the 3 Crucial Questions Seminars, which are sponsored by Bridge Ministries of Detroit, Michigan. The seminars and books are designed to greatly enhance your Christian walk. The following comments will help you appreciate the unique features of the book series.

The 3 Crucial Questions series is based on two fundamental observations. First, there are crucial questions related to the Christian faith for which imperfect Christians seem to have no final answers. Christians living in eternal glory may know fully even as they are known by God, but now we know only in part (1 Cor. 13:12). Therefore, we must ever return to such questions with the prayer that God the Holy Spirit will continue to lead us nearer to "the truth, the whole truth, and nothing but the truth." While recognizing their own frailty, the authors contributing to this series pray that they are thus led.

Second, each Christian generation partly affirms its solidarity with the Christian past by reaffirming "the faith which was once delivered unto the saints" (Jude 3 KJV). Such an affirmation is usually attempted by religious scholars who are notorious for talking only to themselves or by nonexperts whose grasp of the faith lacks depth of insight. Both situations are unfortunate, but we feel that our team of contributing authors is well-prepared to avoid them. Each author is a competent Christian scholar able to share tremendous learning in down-to-earth language both laity and experts can appreciate. In a word, you have in hand a book that is part of a rare series, one that is neither pedantic nor pediatric.

The topics addressed in the series have been chosen for their timelessness, interest level, and importance to Christians everywhere. And the contributing authors are committed to discussing them in a manner that promotes Christian unity. They discuss not only areas of disagreement among Christians but significant areas of agreement as well. Seeking peace and pursuing it as the Bible commands (1 Peter 3:11), they stress common ground on which Christians with different views may meet for wholesome dialogue and reconciliation.

The books in the series consist not merely of printed words; they consist of words to live by. Their pages are filled not only with good information but with sound instruction in successful Christian living. For study is truly Christian only when, in addition to helping us understand our faith, it helps us to live our faith. We pray therefore that you will allow God to use the 3 Crucial Questions series to augment your growth in the grace and knowledge of our Lord and Savior Jesus Christ.

Grant R. Osborne
Richard J. Jones, Jr.

Preface

Very few people would contest that the most influential figure in world history has been Jesus Christ. According to the 1990 Encyclopaedia Britannica *Book of the Year*, adherents of the Christian religion number about 1.76 billion (33.3% of the world's population), with Muslims numbering 935 million (17.7%) and Hindus 705 million (13.3%). No political figure compares with the influence of Jesus Christ.

Persons who wish to disprove Christianity or to undermine the faith of Christians usually focus their critical attention on three matters relating to the person of Jesus. Sometimes they seek to prove that he never existed and is merely a mythical figure. Sometimes they concede his historicity but deny his resurrection from the dead, so that he remains a mortal figure. At other times they attempt to disprove his deity, claiming that he is simply a human figure.

This book addresses these three charges: that Jesus did not exist, that he did not rise from the dead, and that he is not divine. I have attempted to examine the data relevant to these issues with fairness and calmness. Chapters 1 and 2 are apologetic in tone, arguing for the existence and resurrection of Jesus. Chapter 3 sets out the testimony of the New Testament regarding the deity of Jesus Christ and lets the evidence speak for itself. Chapter 2 has a special format.

9

One of the most exciting ways of evaluating evidence is to listen to a group of people formally debating a proposition. Three speakers agree with the proposition as stated and seek to defend it; they are the affirmative side. Three other speakers disagree with the proposition and attempt to discredit it; they form the negative team. In order to treat the historical evidence for the resurrection of Jesus as evenhandedly as possible, I present that evidence in the form of a debate. Hopefully, this will ensure that the arguments both for and against the resurrection of Jesus are offered in their most convincing form.

It will not take the reader long to discover that I am convinced that Jesus Christ is a historical, immortal, and divine figure. Such a conviction can remain a piece of cold intellectual property. On the other hand, it can lead you to call on Jesus Christ for salvation and to bow before him in worship. "Everyone who calls on the name of the Lord will be saved" (Rom. 10:13). And like Thomas of old, we may say to the risen Jesus, "My Lord and my God!" (John 20:28).

Acknowledgments

Warm gratitude is due to Michael Vanlaningham, who, in the midst of doctoral studies, carefully typed the whole manuscript. I am also grateful to Jim Weaver and David Aiken of Baker Book House for expertly guiding this volume through the editorial process.

Permission has been kindly granted by Sheffield Academic Press for the use in chapter 1 of material that first appeared in *Gospel Perspectives*, volume 5: *The Jesus Tradition outside the Gospels* (1985, edited by D. Wenham); and by Zondervan Publishing House to reproduce (in chapter 2) some material that was first published in my book *From Grave to Glory* (1990). Chapter 3 is in part a summary of my 1992 book *Jesus as God: The New Testament Use of Theos in Reference to Jesus* (Baker Book House) and in part an expansion of appendix 2 in that book.

This book is an expansion of lectures that were first delivered in November 1992 as the Berean Lectures in Detroit, Michigan, at the kind invitation of Richard Jones, Director of Bridge Ministries; and then in June 1993 as the Open Lectures in the University of Auckland Conference Centre, generously sponsored by the Bible College of New Zealand and its National Principal, Dr. John Hitchen.

Did Jesus Exist?

istory is full of hoaxes—some humorous, some devilish; some insignificant, some ominous. One of the most humorous and widely publicized hoaxes of this generation involved the work of two British landscape painters, David Chorley and Douglas Bower. Over a period of thirteen years (1978–91) they sneaked around the grainfields of southern England, flattening twenty-five to thirty crops each season into mysterious circles, using a ball of string, a wooden plank, and a baseball cap with a sighting device. Their hoax prompted a rash of explanations. Some thought the circular patterns were the landing spots of UFOs. Others alleged that ball lightning created by atmospheric microwaves had flattened the crops. All this prompted a new science called "cereology" and a new academy called "The Circles Effect Research Unit"![1]

This was a humorous hoax. But what if we were confronted by an ominous hoax? For instance, what if Christianity turned out to be based on a hoax? What if Jesus never existed? After all, almost two thousand years have elapsed since the alleged birth of Jesus. How can we be sure that this remote event ever took place? What if millions of Christians over the centuries simply have been misguided in thinking that Jesus of Nazareth was a historical figure?

It is my intent in this chapter to face this question head-on. We could, of course, immediately turn to the New Testament and examine the evidence of the four Gospels on the matter. But someone could say: "Those documents originated among the early Christians, who had a vested interest in maintaining that their founder was an actual person who lived in first-century Palestine. I will not believe that Christianity has a secure historical basis until you show me independent witnesses—early writers who were not Christians, who had no theological ax to grind, and yet who knew that Jesus was a real person." I accept this challenge as understandable and will now call to the witness stand four non-Christians to give their testimony—one writer of unknown nationality who wrote in Greek and three Roman writers.[2]

Thallus

That the majority of books written in the ancient world have not survived constitutes one of the frustrating facts of history. For instance, not one of the thirty-seven books written by the Roman emperor Claudius is extant. We know of the existence of such lost books through references made to them and quotations from them found in works that have survived. Such is the case of the historian Thallus.[3]

Julius Africanus, who lived about 160–240, was a Christian chronographer who composed a five-volume *History of the World* to A.D. 217. Only fragments of his work survive,

Did Jesus Exist?   15

but in one fragment that describes the earthquake and three-hour darkness that occurred at Jesus' crucifixion, he writes:

> In the third book of his history Thallus calls this darkness an eclipse of the sun—wrongly in my opinion.[4]

According to the early church historian Eusebius, Thallus wrote (in Greek) an account of world history in three books. We cannot be sure when Thallus wrote his *Chronicle*, but it was probably about the middle of the first century A.D.[5]

What can we infer from this fragment of Julius Africanus about the content of Thallus's statement? Clearly, Thallus was not merely claiming that an eclipse of the sun occurred during the reign of Tiberius, as G. A. Wells alleges.[6] Rather, he was speaking of "this darkness," that is, the extraordinary darkness that accompanied the death of Jesus (cf. Luke 23:44–45), and was identifying it as a solar eclipse. If Africanus simply had been questioning the accuracy of Thallus in claiming that an eclipse had occurred at a certain time, he would not have rejected Thallus's view by an expression of opinion: "wrongly in my opinion" or "wrongly it seems to me." Africanus was rejecting a naturalistic explanation of the darkness, not an alleged occurrence of a solar eclipse. He points out that Thallus's explanation was unsatisfactory because an eclipse of the sun is impossible at the time of the full moon. (Jesus was crucified at the time of Passover, which coincides with the full moon.) Clearly, both Thallus and Africanus take it for granted that there had been an unusual darkness at the time of Jesus' crucifixion.

Therefore, Thallus had some knowledge of the Christian tradition regarding the passion of Jesus, and in his *Chroni-*

cle he referred to the preternatural darkness, which he
accepted as a fact but regarded as a phenomenon that could
be explained without invoking the supernatural, as the
Christians did. Obviously, a historian who alluded to and
accepted as reliable the tradition that Christ's death was
accompanied by an unusual darkness also accepted the fact
of Christ's existence. As far as we know, then, Thallus was
the first non-Christian writer to refer to Jesus.

Pliny the Younger

When we come to our next witness, we are dealing
directly with an author's own work, and we have a much
longer passage to consider.

Pliny the Younger (ca. A.D. 61–112) trained in Rome as
a lawyer, practiced in the civil courts, and held a succession
of administrative posts (including a praetorship and con-
sulship). In 110 the emperor Trajan sent him as imperial
legate to restore order in the disorganized province of Bithynia-Pontus. Between 100 and 109 Pliny published nine col-
lections of letters, which ranged in form from personal notes
to short essays. The tenth book of his letters, covering the
years 110–112, contains his official correspondence with
the emperor regarding various administrative problems that
arose in Bithynia-Pontus.

In letter 96 of book 10, penned about 111, Pliny informs
Trajan that he found Christianity to be spreading so quickly
in his province, in both town and country, that temples were
"well-nigh abandoned" and sales of fodder for the sacrificial animals had fallen dramatically. Formal accusations had
been leveled against the Christians, possibly by the aggrieved
tradesmen, and Pliny had presided at the trials. Because the

number of accusations was growing rapidly, he consults with Trajan on several points: whether to discriminate with regard to age; whether the renunciation of Christianity should win indulgence; and whether the very profession of Christianity should be punished or only the "disgraceful practices" that went along with it.[7]

As he reviews his earlier procedure in dealing with anonymous accusations, Pliny informs Trajan that some persons, apparently falsely charged with being Christians, invoked the state gods at his dictation, did reverence to the emperor's image with incense and wine, and also "cursed Christ." Others, who claimed to have previously renounced the Christianity they once professed, also did reverence to the emperor's image and the statues of the gods and "cursed Christ." Pliny continues:

> But they maintained that their guilt or error had amounted only to this: they had been in the habit of meeting on an appointed day before daybreak and singing a hymn antiphonally to Christ as if to a god. (*Epistles* 10:96:7)

This letter, then, contains three references to "Christ" (Latin, *Christus*). Some have suggested that this term here is a title ("Messiah") and not a proper name referring to a person ("Christ").[8] But this is a counsel of despair. What would be the sense of asking any persons, Jews or otherwise, to curse a figure who was simply an object of hope, as proof of recantation? And why would Christians sing an anthem of praise to a Messiah who was merely an expected redeemer and not a historical personage? No evidence exists of a Jewish or Christian messianic cult whose object of worship was a purely mythical figure. No, the "Christ" that certain believers in Pontus were asked to curse was none other than Jesus Christ of Nazareth.

Pliny affirms that these Christians were accustomed to singing a hymn *Christo quasi deo*. Whatever this Latin phrase meant to the one-time Christians who reported the matter to Pliny, Pliny himself would doubtless have understood the phrase in the sense "to Christ as if to a god."[9] If Pliny had regarded Jesus as a god comparable to Asclepius or Osiris, he would have written *Christo deo* or *deo Christo* ("to the god Christ"). The intervening word *quasi* ("as if") highlights the distinctiveness of Jesus in relation to other known gods. In what did that distinctiveness consist? In the fact that, unlike other gods who were worshiped, Christ was a person who had lived on earth.

It is sometimes asserted that this reference to the worship of Christ does not constitute "independent evidence" since Pliny is simply reporting Christian belief.[10] However, this information about the worship of Christ came from persons who had already abandoned the profession of Christianity when they gave their evidence.[11] Such persons would therefore scarcely be likely to create evidence that could prove incriminating to them by suggesting that they had once worshiped a figure not recognized as a state god. What is more, the two earlier references in the letter to "cursing Christ" come from the pen of Pliny, who himself had specified the cursing of Christ as one of the three ways in which Christians might prove they had renounced their allegiance to Christ.

Pliny, then, affords clear testimony to Jesus as a historical figure whose influence was still being felt in the Roman province of Bithynia-Pontus some eighty years after his death.

Tacitus

Our next secular witness to the existence of Jesus may be appropriately described as the ancient world's most distinguished historian.

Cornelius Tacitus was born around A.D. 56 and may have lived until Hadrian's reign (117–138). He served as *consul suffectus* in 97 under Nerva and as proconsul of Asia in 112–113. He authored two major historical works: the *Annals*, which deal with the reigns of Tiberius, Gaius, Claudius, and Nero (14–68) in eighteen books, of which about half are extant, and the *Histories*, covering the period A.D. 69–96 in twelve books, of which only books 1–4 and a section of book 5 have survived.

In the course of describing the events of 64 in book 15 of his *Annals* (written about 115), Tacitus vividly recounts how ten of Rome's fourteen districts were engulfed in disastrous fires that raged for more than six days and outstripped every countermeasure (15:38–40). Because people believed that Nero had grandiose plans to found a new capital and give it his own name (15:40), a rumor spontaneously arose that Nero himself had started the fire. According to Tacitus, the emperor tried to suppress the rumor by diverting the blame for the disaster to the Christians. Self-confessed Christians were arrested and on the basis of information that some of them gave (perhaps under torture), many others were also convicted. All these were "punished with the utmost refinements of cruelty" (15:44).

With regard to these people who were "popularly called 'Christians,' " Tacitus observes that

They got their name from Christ, who had been executed
by sentence of the procurator Pontius Pilate in the reign of
Tiberius. (15:44)

No evidence supports the contention that the passage is
inauthentic. Not only is the style of the whole episode thoroughly Tacitean, but the particular references to Christians
and Christ in the account of the great fire accord with the
context. Tacitus recounts Nero's final ploy to stifle scandal
and regain popular approval. After he had poured the imperial riches into reconstruction, had formulated rigorous
building regulations and fire precautions, and had tried to
appease the gods, he finally "fabricated scapegoats." Also,
Tacitus suggests that, just as execution was the appropriate
fate of the founder of Christianity, so it is the fitting lot of
his followers. Finally, with his concern to trace cause and
effect in history and in particular to trace the origin of
momentous events in seemingly insignificant incidents, Tacitus discloses the origin of this contemptible religious sect
that had gained such remarkable imperial attention in 64.
This "pernicious superstition" had in fact survived the "temporary setback" of the crucifixion of its founder in Judea
in the 30s "only to break out afresh, not only in Judea, the
home of the disease, but in the capital itself" (15:44) in the
60s. And for Tacitus, events that involved Rome and its
emperor were of universal significance, for Rome was the
center of the world and the emperor the center of Rome.

It must remain unlikely that an early Christian forger
would have fabricated a story that involved self-confessed
Christian informers whose treachery led to the conviction
of a "vast multitude" of their fellow Christians. Nor would
a forger have the foremost Roman historian speak of Chris-

tianity so disparagingly. The description of Christians throughout chapter 44 is uniformly scornful and hostile: they are a people "hated for their vices," who have a "hatred of the human race," and whose guilt had earned the ruthless punishment it deserved. Christianity was a "pernicious superstition" needing to be checked, a "disease" to be classed among "all the degraded and shameful things in the world."[12]

Of the three main literary sources for the period of the early Roman Empire, Tacitus surpasses Suetonius and Dio Cassius not only in literary excellence but also in historical accuracy. We may therefore regard as being of special importance his affirmation, registered with what the greatest Tacitean scholar of all time, Sir Ronald Syme, calls "documentary precision,"[13] that Christ was executed under Pontius Pilate and was the founder of a group of sectaries that bore his name.

Suetonius

Finally, I call as witness a Roman polymath whose voluminous writings range over the fields of history, biography, natural history, antiquities, and grammar.

We know relatively little of the life and career of Suetonius. He was probably from Hippo Regius in Numidia (now Annaba in Algeria) and lived from about A.D. 69 until the 130s. For a short period, perhaps 119–121, he served as secretary to the emperor Hadrian. The only work that has been nearly wholly preserved is his *Lives of the Caesars*, the biographies of Julius Caesar and the first eleven Roman emperors down to Domitian, published about 120.

Book 5 of his *Lives* is entitled "The Deified Claudius." In the course of a rather prosaic enumeration of the administrative acts of Claudius at home and abroad, Suetonius makes this statement:

> He [Claudius] expelled the Jews from Rome, because of the rioting in which they were constantly engaging at the instigation of Chrestus (*impulsore Chresto*). (25:4)

Rarely has the authenticity of this passage been called into question, for it contains two patent inaccuracies—the spelling *Chrestus* for *Christus* (assuming the allusion is to Christ) and the assumption that Christ, as the ringleader of the rioters, was living in Rome during the reign of Claudius (41–54). What are we to make of these inaccuracies in Suetonius or his source?

There are several compelling considerations that support the prevailing view that *Chrestus* refers to Jesus Christ.[14] First, *Chrestus* was a common and natural misspelling of *Christus*.[15] The substitution of "e" for "i" was a common error in the spelling of proper names.[16] Second, if Suetonius had been referring to some unknown Jewish agitator or Christian leader called *Chrestus*, he would have written "at the instigation of a *certain* Chrestus" (*impulsore Chresto quodam*). The absence of the word *certain* (*quodam*) indicates that Suetonius expected his readers to be able to identify the person to whom he was referring. Only one *Chrestus* would fit that category in 120 when Suetonius was writing—the *Chrestus* whose followers were popularly known as *Chrestiani* ("Christians"). Third, an unexplained passing allusion to the founder of Christianity would be natural for a writer who elsewhere refers to Christians. In his *Life of Nero* (16:2) Suetonius notes that under Nero "punishment was inflicted on the Christians, a class of people given to a new and mischievous superstition." Finally, early in the fourth century the Latin Christian Lactantius speaks of "the error of the ignorant, who by the change of a letter are accustomed to call him [Jesus] Chrestus."[17]

The erroneous assumption that Christ himself was in Rome at the time of the riots betrays the second inaccuracy in Suetonius. These riots may have been violent demonstrations by Roman Jews against the burgeoning Christian community in Rome, but more probably they were violent disputes between Jews and Christians concerning the claim being pressed by Christian missionaries that Jesus of Nazareth was in fact the Jewish Messiah, disputes comparable to those marking Paul's missionary activity.[18] Unlike his close friend Herod Agrippa I, who saw a clear difference between Jewish Christianity and normative Judaism (Acts 12:1–4), Claudius evidently regarded the riots as a purely Jewish affair or else did not deem it necessary to distinguish between Christianity and Judaism in legal proceedings and therefore directed his expulsion order against "all the Jews" (Acts 18:2) in Rome, Christian and non-Christian alike. The edict of Claudius mentioned in the sentence of Suetonius may be dated in the year 49.[19] We know that Christ was executed in Jerusalem in 30 or perhaps 33, so how could Suetonius place Christ in Rome in 49? Perhaps he was simply faithfully reproducing a source that was unaware of the Christian reference and therefore unreliable on this point (it was typical of Suetonius to quote his sources verbatim, whether they were in Greek or Latin, in verse or in prose). Alternatively, "if his sources indicated that the riots which provoked Claudius's edict of expulsion were due to the

introduction and propagation of Christianity in the capital,
he could well have drawn the mistaken inference that it had
been introduced there by Christ in person."[20] But this error
does not invalidate the reference to Christ. Clearly, Suetonius or his source (possibly an earlier historian's version of
the riots, based on local police records) viewed Christ as a
historical person, capable of fomenting unrest.

For all its difficulties, this reference in Suetonius points
to Jesus as the leader of a band of dissident Jews, if not the
founder of Christianity.

Objections Considered

Before we draw our overall conclusions to this chapter,
we must consider two general objections to this evidence.
The first objection claims that if the Jesus who is described
in the four Gospels had really existed, he would surely have
been noticed by more than four early non-Christian writers and at greater length than in the extremely brief extant
references to him.

It should be noted, in the first place, that our knowledge
of any aspect of first-century history depends on comparatively few witnesses, witnesses that themselves are fragmen-
tary. Second, Roman writers could hardly be expected to
have foreseen the subsequent influence of Christianity in the
Roman Empire and therefore to have carefully documented
the beginnings of this new religion in the appearance of a
Nazarene prophet. On the contrary, as M. Goguel observes,

> For the whole of Roman society in the first century,
> Christianity was merely a contemptible Eastern superstition.
> It was ignored, save when it proved the occasion of political
> and social ferment. It is from this point of view alone that

the Latin authors speak of it, and it is natural that they should not take the trouble to collect and examine the real or fictitious traditions to which those whom they regarded as agitators referred.[21]

Third, for all its political turbulence, the Roman province of Judea was in a remote corner of the empire that was of little intrinsic importance to Rome. The summary execution of a messianic agitator in Judea would not have been an exceptional occurrence that was worthy of special notice. Josephus tells us that "about two thousand" Jewish insurgents were crucified by the legate of Syria, Quintilius Varus, following the widespread disturbances after the death of Herod the Great in 4 B.C.[22]

Behind the call for additional non-Christian witnesses to the existence of Jesus is the refusal to accept the testimony of the four writers we do have. Should we reject the four because they are not forty? The silence of the imaginary majority cannot overthrow the clear testimony of the few. This demand for other witnesses reminds me of the anecdote about a man accused of theft. At his trial the prosecuting attorney brought forward four witnesses who saw him commit the crime, while the defense attorney introduced as evidence fourteen persons who did not see him do it. Needless to say, the man was found guilty! We have four extrabiblical witnesses who testify that Jesus really existed. Why should we disbelieve them in favor of four or fourteen who do not refer to Jesus? We might also observe at this point that none of the Greek or Roman authors of the first century (except Thallus) would have had reason to refer to Jesus, if we may judge from the scope and purpose of their writings.[23] Thallus, on the other hand, is distinctive in this effort to show the points of contact between Greco-Roman and Oriental history.

This leads naturally to the second objection to be considered, which claims that there is no contemporary non-Christian writer who testifies to the existence of Jesus.

I will concede that not one of our four early witnesses, with the possible exception of Thallus (his dates are unknown), was a contemporary of Jesus. Thallus probably belonged to the middle of the first century, while Pliny, Tacitus, and Suetonius wrote in the early second century. This call for a contemporary witness, however, is wholly artificial with regard to the distant past, when historians were few in number. Even if a writer was not contemporary with the events he described, his record would be accurate if his sources were reliable and he used them responsibly.

The point may be illustrated by reference to the best-known contemporary of Jesus—the emperor Tiberius, who ruled from 14 to 37. Our knowledge of his reign, which is recognized on all sides to be accurate, derives primarily from four Roman sources. The least satisfactory is actually a contemporary record written about 30 by the amateur historian Velleius Paterculus, whereas the most valuable sources for the life of Tiberius date from some eighty to two hundred years later: the *Annals* of Tacitus (ca. 115), the life of Tiberius by Suetonius (ca. 120), and the Roman history of Dio Cassius (ca. 230).[24] (Two of these three writers, Tacitus and Suetonius, refer to Jesus.) That the best testimony regarding the principate of Tiberius Caesar dates from the two subsequent centuries does not mean that he is a figment of scholars' imagination. So also in the case of the itinerant rabbi from Nazareth: that no contemporary non-

Christian writers mention him does not prove that he never existed.

Conclusions

Four early classical authors witness to the existence of a historical person called Christ: Thallus, Pliny the Younger, Tacitus, and Suetonius. True, some modern writers have raised specific and general objections to this conclusion, but their efforts to discount the evidence remain totally unconvincing.

These four classical writers also provide some information about the life and influence of Jesus, information that accords with the testimony of the New Testament. We may summarize the data in six points and indicate a selection of New Testament passages that are thus corroborated.

1. Tacitus: Christ attracted sufficient attention to be arraigned before the procurator of Judea (Matt. 27:11–26; Mark 15:1–15; Luke 23:1–7; John 18:28–19:16; 1 Tim. 6:13), who condemned him to death (Matt. 27:26; Mark 15:15; Luke 23:23–24; John 19:16).

2. Tacitus: Christ was executed by crucifixion (Matt. 27:35, 50; Mark 15:24; Luke 23:33, 46; John 19:18, 30) while Pilate was procurator of Judea (26–36) and Tiberius was emperor (14–37) (cf. Luke 3:1). We may therefore assume that Jesus lived in Judea early in the first century A.D.

3. Thallus: A preternatural darkness occurred at the time of the crucifixion (Matt. 27:45; Mark 15:33; Luke 23:44–45).

4. Tacitus: Christ attracted a group of followers (Luke 6:13–16; 10:1; Acts 1:13–15) who by the time of Nero were sufficiently numerous and despised (1 Pet. 1:1; 4:12–16) to be held accountable for the great fire of Rome.

5. Tacitus: Christ's followers derived their name, "Christians," from him (Acts 11:26; 26:28; 1 Pet. 4:16). Seutonius: This indicates his role as founder (or "instigator") of a distinctive sect arising within Judaism (Luke 23:2–3; Acts 24:5).

6. Pliny the Younger: Some eighty years after Christ's death, Christians in Bithynia-Pontus regularly addressed him as a deity (cf. John 20:28; 1 Pet. 1:1; 3:15).

To summarize the data in more general terms, two of the four authors describe certain circumstances of Jesus' death, one referring to the responsibility of the local governor for his execution (Tacitus), the other mentioning the extraordinary darkness occurring at the time (Thallus). The other two writers allude to Jesus' influence, either as the leader of a religious sect associated with rioting (Suetonius) or as the object of his followers' worship (Pliny).

But does the Christian faith need a historical Jesus? Does the non-Christian testimony to Jesus really matter?

The answer to both questions must assuredly be "Yes!" If historians were to prove beyond reasonable doubt that Jesus never existed, human beings might still have a convenient or attractive object for their vague faith, but Christianity as such would be reduced to mere fancy, for the Christ whom the apostles proclaimed was the resurrected Jesus of Nazareth. As Paul would have expressed it, "If Jesus never lived, our preaching is useless and so is your faith."[25] Such a discovery would not simply be a theological embarrassment or inconvenience; it would be a religious catastrophe, the death-knell of historic Christianity. As matters stand, however, the most significant historical evidence outside the New Testament does in fact validate the four Gospels on this basic issue of the existence of Jesus of Nazareth. Christians are not devotees of some mythical figure created by human artistry out of the fabric of folklore and legend but are followers of a historical person, a Nazarene artisan and wandering rabbi of the first century A.D. who was crucified during the reign of Tiberius and, as the subsequent chapters will argue, rose from the dead and inherently shares the nature of God himself.

Did Jesus Rise
from the Dead?

Chairperson

Welcome to this special centennial meeting of the Debating Society of Oxford University. The proposition to be debated this evening is this: "That Jesus Christ did not rise from the dead." Our three speakers for the affirmative are, in order of speaking, Philip Carter, who captains the team, Janice Miller, and Eugene Sanderson. For the negative, who will be arguing that Jesus did rise from the dead, we have team captain Alice Johnson, Daryl Hildebrandt, and Susan Adams. Each speaker will have ten minutes, then each captain will have three minutes to draw conclusions. Now to the debate.[1]

First Speaker for the Affirmative—"That Jesus Christ Did Not Rise from the Dead": Philip Carter

No one can contest that the early Christians attached supreme importance to the resurrection of Christ. It was at the heart of their message to the world. As the Book of Acts attests (4:33; 17:18), whether they were preaching the Good News in Jerusalem or in Athens, its essence was the resurrection. In 1 Corinthians 15:3–8 Paul identifies the four pillars on which the Christian faith is built: the death, burial, resurrection, and appearances of Jesus. We agree with Paul—and the negative side—that without the resurrection the New Testament loses its soul and the Christian faith forfeits its central pillar. Without a risen Christ, the Christian message becomes meaningless and the Christian's faith futile. As 1 Corinthians 15:14 declares, "If Christ has not been raised, our preaching is useless and so is your faith." We agree! and will try to show that the faith of Christians in a resurrected Jesus *is* useless, that here we are confronted with a gigantic hoax. Christianity is based on a myth, and Christians have been hoodwinked.

Let me begin by explaining this myth of the empty tomb, which constitutes such a prominent feature of all defenses of the resurrection. Two German scholars early in the nineteenth century gave the definitive explanation. C. H. G. Venturini in his *Natürliche Geschichte des grossen Prophet von Nazareth* (*Natural History of the Great Prophet from Nazareth*) (1800) and H. E. G. Paulus in his *Das Leben Jesu* (*The Life of Jesus*) (1828) showed conclusively that Jesus swooned on the cross, was taken for dead, but after burial revived in the cool atmosphere of the sepulcher, escaped from the tomb, and "appeared" to his disciples, who were convinced that he had risen from the dead.

The most recent exponent of a similar view is J. D. M. Derrett, formerly Professor of Oriental Laws in the University of London. He shows that in reference to Jesus' own experience the Greek word *anastasis* means "revival" in a

physical sense, not "resurrection" in a theological sense.
Derrett states, "The religious belief in Resurrection was
forcibly hooked onto a historical *anastasis* of an individual."
Distinguishing brain death from clinical death, that is, the
apparent cessation of breathing and pulse, Derrett maintains that in the coolness of the tomb Jesus revived from the
clinical death he had experienced on the cross, a death that
had been "masked, perhaps, by a self-induced trance." But
he survived only briefly before gangrene and high fever led
to his collapse and brain death. His disciples probably cre-
mated his body in the Place of Burning in the Kedron Val-
ley, where his ashes would have become indistinguishable
from the remains of innumerable Passover animals.[2] So Derrett believes that Jesus suffered clinical death, but not real
death, then revived, and subsequently experienced brain
death or real death; and that his disciples chose to interpret
that temporary revival as actual resurrection.

I have here in my hand a modern example that illustrates
how easily a belief can arise that a person who was thought
to be dead later revived. The front page of the *Weekly World
News* on August 21, 1990, bore the stunning heading "JFK
IS ALIVE!" The newspaper printed excerpts from a letter by
a Polish neurosurgeon, Dr. Sonya Faron, who claimed that
President Kennedy survived the attempt on his life in Dal-
las in 1963 and has been living in a secret convalescence
center in Poland ever since. In this unsolicited letter to the
News, dated June 11, 1990, Dr. Faron writes:

> The story I am about to relate to you is fact. John Fitzgerald
> Kennedy, the 35th president of the United States, was not
> assassinated in 1963. He is alive in Poland. He was brought
> here to prevent a second assassination attempt after his

wounding by the assassin Oswald. He has been under CIA guard since. I know because I was Mr. Kennedy's personal physician from 1963 to 1989. . . . Mr. Kennedy suffered brain damage. He was left paralyzed from the waist down. But he is still lucid and has remained involved in American politics since his alleged death and mock funeral in 1963.

The article in the *News* continues:

> According to Dr. Faron: Kennedy knew that an attempt on his life was likely and personally made arrangements to go into hiding when and if the assassination was attempted. The doctor stopped short of saying that Kennedy knew who wanted to kill him. But the President apparently believed that the assassin or assassins would not give up until they were successful.
>
> To prevent a second attempt on his life Kennedy was jetted to a convalescence center in Poland a few days after he was shot and a wax likeness was buried at Arlington National Cemetery. At least 16 politicians and businessmen as well as the CIA were in on the deception.

Now this letter is clearly a hoax. We all know that Kennedy died in November 1963. He did die, and dead people don't rise. The Gospels that speak of Jesus being alive were also hoaxes, the difference in their case being that Jesus did not die when his disciples thought, but later.

But, for the sake of argument, let us imagine that Jesus experienced real death upon the cross and that after an interval his tomb was found to be empty. As I see it, there are three perfectly plausible explanations of the empty tomb.

First, the claim of the women to have found the tomb of Jesus empty is itself empty, because they returned to the wrong tomb. This is how the point is made by Kirsopp Lake, an eminent American New Testament scholar:

> It is seriously a matter for doubt whether the women were really in a position to be quite certain that the tomb which they visited was that in which they had seen Joseph of Arimathea bury the Lord's body. The neighborhood of Jerusalem is full of rock tombs, and it would not be easy to distinguish one from another without careful notes. . . . It is very doubtful if they were close to the tomb at the moment of burial. . . . It is likely that they were watching from a distance, and that Joseph of Arimathea was a representative of the Jews rather than of the disciples. If so, they would have had but a limited power to distinguish between one rock tomb and another close to it. The possibility, therefore, that they came to the wrong tomb is to be reckoned with, and it is important because it supplies the natural explanation of the fact that whereas they had seen the tomb closed, they found it open. . . .
>
> If it were not the same, the circumstances all seem to fall into line. The women came in the early morning to a tomb which they thought was the one in which they had seen the Lord buried. They expected to find a closed tomb, but they found an open one; and a young man, . . . guessing their errand, tried to tell them that they had made a mistake in the place. "He is not here," said he, "see the place where they laid him," and probably pointed to the next tomb. But the women were frightened at the detection of their errand, and fled.[3]

A second explanation of the empty tomb is this. The body of Jesus was stolen from the tomb, probably by his disciples, who, thoroughly dispirited, desperately wanted a message to preach and so stole the body and then corporately agreed to announce Jesus' resurrection. Or perhaps the Jews themselves executed the theft, in their eagerness to "strangle Christianity in the cradle," so to speak, or to prevent the tomb from becoming a place of pilgrimage for Jesus' followers. Or again, the removal of the body may have been performed by Joseph of Arimathea, the owner of the grave, who had carried out the burial as the Gospels say, but who, on reflection, was loath to have his respectable family tomb occupied by the body of a crucified man, so he secretly removed the corpse to a permanent grave. Obviously, various sets of people would have had understandable motives for removing Jesus' crucified body from the sepulcher. No detective investigating this case of grave robbery would have been left guessing the motives for the crime.

Finally, I would suggest that the empty-tomb tradition might have been a legend created by the church at a comparatively late stage to substantiate its claim that there were witnesses of the risen Jesus. Or perhaps it was an effort to express in material terms an originally spiritual understanding of Christ's resurrection as God's victory through the cross of Christ. Either way, the story of an empty tomb belongs to the category of legend or myth.

First Speaker for the Negative—It Is Not True "That Jesus Christ Did Not Rise from the Dead": Alice Johnson

I am glad, Mr. Carter, that you began with one point on which our two teams agree—that "Jesus Christ, risen from the dead" (2 Tim. 2:8), is the focal point of the New Testament and of Christianity. It is my purpose to demonstrate that the Christian faith and the resurrection of Jesus *are* firmly based in history; as firmly based, for example, as the assassinations of Julius Caesar in 44 B.C. and J. F. Kennedy in 1963 or the death of some six million Jews in the Holocaust.

Now to take up your points. First, the so-called swoon theory. Even in the sophisticated modern guise proposed by Professor Derrett, the theory totally fails to explain the facts.

First, quite apart from the uniform testimony of the New Testament that Jesus actually died and his corpse was placed in a tomb,[4] there is unambiguous evidence outside the New Testament that testifies to the actual death of Jesus. The Roman historian, Tacitus, in book 15 of his *Annals*, written about 115, notes that the Christians "got their name from Christ, who had been executed by sentence of the procurator Pontius Pilate in the reign of Tiberius" (15:44).

Second, under no circumstances could Jesus have recovered from the Roman scourging (Mark 15:15) and crucifixion (Mark 15:24), not to speak of the lance thrust (John 19:34), as quickly as this theory demands. Moreover, the purpose of the lance thrust was to ensure that the victim was actually dead. And, on this view, how are we to explain Pilate's careful cross-questioning of the centurion about the relative speed of Jesus' death before he released the corpse for burial (Mark 15:42–45)?

Third, how could a recently crucified man, desperately needing medical attention, have created the impression on his disconsolate followers that he had conquered death and was worthy of worship (Matt. 28:16–20; John 20:19–29)?

Of course your analogy of the Kennedy case, fascinating as it was, falls down at the crucial point, for you were suggesting that Jesus did not immediately die, but Kennedy did, as you admitted.

Did the women visit the wrong tomb? Is Lake's theory valid? He appeals to the words of Mark 16:6, where the "young man" addressed the women: " 'Don't be alarmed,' he said. 'You are looking for Jesus the Nazarene, who was crucified. He has risen! He is not here. See the place where they laid him.' " Lake's view demands that the reference to the resurrection ("he has risen") be arbitrarily omitted from this verse; that Mark's statement (15:47) that Mary Magdalene and Mary the mother of Joses had seen where Jesus was buried be discounted; that the *neaniskos* ("young man") be taken as a reference to a caretaker or gardener, whereas Mark's description of him as "dressed in a white robe" (see Rev. 6:11; 7:9, 13) and as giving the divine message (Mark 16:6–7) shows that he regarded him as an angel (compare Matt. 28:5); and that the women and the young man remained silent about the true explanation of the empty tomb. In any case, if the women mistook the tomb because they arrived in semi-darkness, it was too dark for any gardener or caretaker to be working. If it was full light they would not have mistaken the tomb.

Was the body stolen? The difficulties confronting this view are insurmountable. How did the disciples manage to elude or overpower the guard of Jewish temple police posted at the tomb precisely to prevent such a robbery (Matt. 27:62–66)? Why would anyone stealing the body bother to unwind and then fold or rewind the several yards of linen cloth that encircled the corpse (see John 20:6–7)? Moreover, it is difficult enough to believe that dispirited disciples who were oblivious of Jesus' predictions of his resurrection (Mark 8:31–32; Luke 24:6–8, 11) would fix on the desperate plan of stealing the body, of vowing never to divulge the truth, and of proclaiming his resurrection. But it stretches credulity beyond the limit to believe that men were willing to suffer and die for what they knew to be a gigantic hoax and that the truth never slipped out, even to other followers of Jesus. Instead of a physical miracle—the resurrection of Jesus from the tomb—we are asked to accept a psychological miracle.

If certain Jews or Joseph of Arimathea as a member of the Sanhedrin (Mark 15:43) stole the body, they would have created the very rumors they were anxious to prevent and would have been able to refute the Christian assertion that Jesus was alive by producing his corpse, or at least the person who carried out the theft. If, on the other hand, Joseph acted as a secret disciple (see John 19:38) and transferred the body from a temporary to a permanent grave after the Sabbath, why did he choose to do this legitimate task in the darkness and why did he not inform the disciples?

Is the empty-tomb tradition legendary? We should note that neither Acts nor the Epistles contain any hint that in their earliest preaching Christians proclaimed the resurrection as a spiritual victory without relating it to the bodily resurrection of Jesus. On the contrary, to judge by our sources, the resurrection was proclaimed as victory precisely because death was thereby forced to release its grip on the body of Jesus (Acts 2:24–32; 13:34–37; and also Rev. 1:17–18). In addition, if the empty-tomb tradition was a fabrication for apologetic purposes, it is curious that so many apparent discrepancies between the four records were left "undoctored," and that the reactions of the disciples to the discovery of the empty tomb were portrayed as fear in Matthew 28:5, 8, trembling astonishment in Mark 16:8, perplexity in Luke 24:4, and mocking disbelief in Luke 24:11. Also, this view leaves us with the problem of the disposal of Jesus' body. If in fact his enemies placed him in a common grave,[5] and the place where he was buried was forgotten, how are we to account for the burial tradition found in all four Gospels that associates Joseph of Arimathea with the entombing of Jesus, or for the Jewish silence about the case when the Christians publicly claimed that the "God of Abraham, Isaac, and Jacob" had contradicted the Jewish rejection of Jesus by raising him from the dead, as Acts 2:23–24; 3:13–15 asserts?

Let me conclude by sketching the evidence for the empty tomb. First, *the tradition of the empty tomb is recorded in all four Gospels.* It is true that multiple attestation is no proof of truth. A falsehood does not become true by being repeated four times. But what is significant about the Gospels' tradition concerning the empty tomb is that it reflects three or four *independent* strands of material, namely, Mark 16:1–8, Matthew 28:11–15 (considered to be special material not found in Mark or Luke), John 20:11–18, and probably Luke 24:1–12. When we remember that countless "facts" of ancient history rest on the testimony of a single literary witness, this fourfold literary testimony to the emptiness of the tomb becomes a powerful argument.

Second, *the earliest Christians could not have continued to proclaim the resurrection of Jesus in the city of Jerusalem or have continued to survive there as a community, unless the tomb had been empty.* It is inconceivable, that when the Christians publicly claimed in Jerusalem that "the God of Abraham and of Isaac and of Jacob" had overturned the Jewish rejection of Jesus by raising him from the dead, the Jerusalem Jews would have maintained a conspiracy of silence if they had proof that the tomb was still occupied or could produce witnesses who could account for the disappearance and disposal of the body. The bold and startling claim of the Christians would have collapsed if someone in the audience could retort, "We know where Jesus was buried, and we have checked—the tomb is still intact"; or, "Here are witnesses who know the whereabouts of Jesus' body." The claim that the tomb was empty was open to what some call "empirical falsification." The point is this: "The silence of the Jews is as significant as the speech of the Christians."[6]

Third, *in their polemic against the early Christians, the Jews assumed the empty tomb.* Matthew 28:11–15 recounts a transaction between the guards who had been sent to watch Jesus' tomb and the Jewish authorities:

> While the women were on their way, some of the guards went into the city and reported to the chief priests everything that had happened. When the chief priests had met with the elders and devised a plan, they gave the soldiers a large sum of money, telling them, "You are to say, 'His disciples came during the night and stole him away while we were asleep.' If this report gets to the governor, we will satisfy him and keep you out of trouble." So the soldiers took the money and did as they were instructed. And this story has been widely circulated among the Jews to this very day.

The last sentence indicates that at the time Matthew wrote his Gospel many Jews were seeking to counteract Christian assertions about Jesus by claiming that the empty tomb was the result of "body snatching." This explanation presupposes that the tomb was indeed empty. Evidently this Jewish counterclaim continued to have currency throughout the second century and beyond, for both Justin Martyr, who wrote about 155, in his *Dialogue with Trypho* (108) and Tertullian, about 200, in his *The Shows* (30) accuse the Jews of their day of charging that Jesus' disciples had stolen his body. We cannot doubt the accuracy of this testimony of Matthew, Justin, and Tertullian, for they are writing as Christians and therefore recording what amounts to "hostile" evidence.

Fourth, *the early Christians, as Jews, would have assumed that resurrection shortly after death implied an empty tomb*. To Jews of the first century A.D., any idea of a resurrection shortly after death involved at least the emptying of a tomb or grave and the revival of the physical body. The Jewish contemporaries of Jesus knew that Lazarus could not be raised from the dead until first the stone that lay over his burial cave had been removed (see John 11:38–44). No one could be regarded as resurrected shortly after death while his corpse lay in a tomb. So the early Christian claim that Jesus was alive necessarily implied that his body was no longer entombed. Accordingly, when Paul asserts, on the one hand, that Jesus was laid in a tomb (Acts 13:29) or was buried (1 Cor. 15:4a) and, on the other, that he had been raised from the dead (Acts 13:30; 1 Cor. 15:4b), he is implying that the sepulcher in which he had been buried was empty.

Finally, *there is no evidence that the tomb of Jesus was venerated*. The Jews of ancient times venerated the burial places of prophets and other holy persons such as righteous martyrs (Matt. 23:29; Acts 2:29; 1 Macc. 13:25–30). It is therefore remarkable that the early Christians gave no particular attention to the tomb of Jesus, for they regarded their master as no ordinary prophet or holy man but as the Son of God. Remarkable, that is, unless his tomb was empty.

Here, then, we have a formidable array of arguments that cumulatively put it beyond reasonable doubt that the tomb of Jesus was discovered to be empty early on a Sunday morning some thirty-six hours after his burial. So the question remains: Who emptied the tomb?

Second Speaker for the Affirmative: Janice Miller

My colleague, Mr. Carter, has dealt more than adequately with the matter of the empty tomb. I would merely add to his penetrating remarks that in itself an empty tomb proves nothing more than that the tomb is empty! After all, if a corpse were to go missing from a mortuary, the empty mortuary would be in itself no evidence of resurrection. There may be a simpler, more natural explanation. A necrophiliac has been at work! For the Christian case to hold water, they must show that the purported appearances of Jesus—alive and well—were actual and not imaginary. So I shall begin my presentation by showing that these so-called appearances were purely psychological phenomena—real, but purely in the mind. The French theologian and Orientalist Joseph Renan (1823–92) argued this case persuasively last century:

> The so-called appearances of the Risen Christ were due to the excited state of mind in which the disciples were after the death of their Master. Overwrought and mentally distraught by the shock of His death, and yearning for His presence, they saw apparitions or visions of Him. But these were purely subjective—phantasms or mental hallucinations. They longed to see Him; they expected to see Him; and they thought they did see Him. Their thought was perfectly

honest, but it was nevertheless a hallucination. For persons in a state of unusual mental excitement and expectancy, especially when they are also of a highly strung nervous temperament, such visions are, it is represented, common phenomena of religious history, and are often contagious. So it was in the case of the appearances of Jesus. They began with the women, probably with Mary Magdalene, an excitable and nervous person. Her story that she had seen the Lord was eagerly embraced; it spread with lightning rapidity, and with the force of an epidemic. What she believed she had seen others believed they too must see, and they saw. The visions were the product of their dwelling in fond and affectionate memory on the personality of their Master, which, after the first shock of despair was over, they came to feel was such that He must have survived death.[7]

But it is also possible that the disciples experienced objective visions. In this case we can appeal to the authority of Karl Keim (1825–78), the Protestant rationalist who authored three massive volumes entitled *Die Geschichte Jesu von Nazara* (*The History of Jesus of Nazareth*) (1867–72). He suggests that the appearances "were not purely subjective—the result of the enthusiasm and mental excitement of the disciples—but real, objectively caused manifestations of the Risen Christ." His theory is that, "while the body of the Crucified Jesus remained in the tomb, His living spirit sent telegrams to the disciples to assure them that He still lived, telegrams or supernatural manifestations which the disciples took for *bona fide* bodily appearances of their Risen Master."[8] So we can rest assured that adequate explanations of the so-called appearances of Jesus were given over a hundred years ago by French and German theologians.

Moving on now from the appearances, I draw your attention to the dramatic discrepancies between the four Gospels in their records of the resurrection. Take, for example, the alleged duration of the appearances: in Matthew and Luke they last one day; in John eight days or so; in Acts forty days. As for location, in Matthew, Mark, and John 21 they occur in Galilee; in Luke and John 20, in Jerusalem. As for the number of appearances, Matthew lists two, Luke five, and John four, while Mark, in the shorter ending, which is probably original, omits them altogether! Or think of the persons the women found at the tomb: in Matthew one angel, in Mark a young man, in Luke two men, in John two angels. And so on. This spectacular disagreement between allegedly reliable sources of information shows in fact how unreliable they are! Not surprisingly, the twentieth-century German theologian Willi Marxsen arrived at the verdict "that the stories contradict one another, that they cannot be harmonized and that they therefore cannot be historical."[9]

If we think, for a moment, of the resurrection stories as a whole, we are quite clearly in the fantasy land of Peter Pan, the land of charming mythology—with angels appearing on earth, stones rolling away, and earthquakes occurring at the psychological moment. After all, the very idea of resurrection is a religious myth that Christianity borrowed from other ancient religions to appeal to a clientele accustomed to gods who died and rose. In his classic 1906 work, *The Golden Bough*, Sir James Frazer amassed evidence to show that in the ancient world there was a widespread worship of a dying and rising god—Tammuz in Mesopotamia, Adonis in Syria, Attis in Asia Minor, Osiris in Egypt—and, we can add, Jesus in Judea.

To illustrate my point about mythology, let me read the account of the resurrection in the Gospel of Peter (35–42), which dates from the mid-second century:

> Now in the night in which the Lord's day dawned, when the soldiers, two by two in every watch, were keeping guard, there rang out a loud voice in heaven, and they saw the heavens opened and two men come down from there in a great brightness and draw nigh to the sepulchre. That stone which had been laid against the entrance to the sepulchre started of itself to roll and gave way to the side, and the sepulchre was opened, and both the young men entered in. When now those soldiers saw this, they awakened the centurion and the elders—for they also were there to assist at the watch. And whilst they were relating what they had seen, they saw again three men come out from the sepulchre, and two of them sustaining the other, and a cross following them, and the heads of the two reaching to heaven, but that of him who was led of them by the hand overpassing the heavens. And they heard a voice out of the heavens crying, "Thou hast preached to them that sleep," and from the cross there was heard the answer, "Yea."[10]

How utterly "fantastic"! Two men descending from heaven, a stone rolling by itself, heads reaching to or into heaven, a walking and talking cross!

Second Speaker for the Negative: Daryl Hildebrandt

I have been writing furiously, Ms. Miller, trying to keep up with you, so that I can respond to each of your points—appearances, discrepancies, mythology.

If the appearances were *subjective visions*, as Renan proposes, we would have expected the disciples to be in a psychological condition that was conducive to hallucinations. But so far from being full of expectancy and absorbed in meditative prayer, the disciples who earlier had misunderstood Jesus' prophecies regarding his resurrection had gathered behind locked doors for fear of the Jews, as John 20:19 tells us. They had gloomy faces (Luke 24:17; cf. John 20:11) because the crucifixion had shattered their fondest messianic hopes (Luke 24:19–21). What is more, they greeted the first news of the resurrection as "utter nonsense" (Luke 24:11). Alternatively, if the hallucinations were induced by physical conditioning such as prolonged lack of food and sleep, how are we to explain the continuation of the visions for forty days (Acts 1:3)? When a person has a visual hallucination, he or she perceives patterns of light or objects that are not recognizable by any other persons present. It is an individual, private occurrence. But the Gospels record "appearances" to groups at different times and in various places: two on the road to Emmaus in the afternoon, seven beside the sea of Galilee in the morning, ten in a house in the evening. And, with regard to Jesus' appearance to over five hundred people on a single occasion, we may ask whether simultaneous, identical hallucinations are psychologically feasible. Moreover, hallucinations may account for sight, but not for sound. In the resurrection narratives the words of the risen Jesus figure prominently. He is both seen and heard. And why the initial difficulty in recognizing Jesus on at least three occasions (Luke 24:13–31; John 20:14–15; 21:4)? Why the abrupt halt to the visions after forty days?

Now, regarding Keim's suggestion that Jesus induced *objective visions* of himself in the consciousness of his disciples to convince them that his resurrection was a spiritual reality—if Jesus in fact sent such "telegrams from heaven" (as they have been called), he can scarcely be acquitted of deception, for what the disciples saw (on this view), namely Jesus in some recognizable and therefore bodily form, was not actually true, for Jesus' body was decaying in some grave in Jerusalem or else had been disposed of by burning. Nor does this view fit with the auditory and kinetic aspects of the appearances. It seems that Jesus never remained silent or motionless when he appeared but engaged in actions such as walking, talking, teaching, preparing food, and eating.

Regarding the *alleged discrepancies*, we should immediately acknowledge that it is very difficult to harmonize all the details into a single account, but it is possible, and many reconstructions have been made.[11] That no two efforts at harmonization totally agree is a testimony not to the contradictory nature of the evidence but merely to the paucity of the data and the lack of collusion among the witnesses. Indeed, we could argue that the very difficulty of harmonizing the accounts shows their reliability, for fabricated stories would tend to be harmonized before publication. One final point should be made. Even if there were contradictions between the resurrection narratives, the bodily resurrection of Jesus from the grave would not be thereby disproved. I may illustrate this point thus. Among the ancient writers who record the circumstances of the great fire of Rome of A.D. 64, disagreement exists about the precise whereabouts of Nero when he "fiddled" while Rome burned. Tacitus places him on the stage of his private theater, Suetonius locates the exhibition in the tower of Maecenas, whereas Dio Cassius says it took place on the palace roof.[12] Yet, for all these irreconcilable differences, no historian of the principate of Nero doubts that he played the lyre and sang while the city was ablaze.

Mythology. There are certainly some similarities between the Gospels and redeemer myths in other religions, but Frazer's case has been shown to be fragile, since it is based on imprecise and superficial parallels, often from post-Christian sources. For example, among the gods you mentioned, only Osiris of Egypt was "raised" from death, and that was by his wife Isis in a reanimation leading to life among the dead, where he reigns as a mummy, so that his "new life" is merely a replica of earthly life. But, according to the New Testament, Jesus was raised from among the dead by God, his Father, in a transformed body to reign over both the living and the dead from his heavenly throne.[13] That is, the differences far outweigh any similarities and point to a totally different origin for the Gospel narratives— an origin rooted in history. No other religion in the world— past or present—claims that its founder was a divine being who walked this earth as a fully human person, who died, and who returned to life and appeared on earth before returning to heaven.

In conclusion, let me give four reasons why we can rely on the accuracy of the Gospel accounts of the resurrection and of Jesus' appearances.

First, *all four resurrection narratives have "the ring of truth."* The reader cannot help being impressed by the extraordinary sobriety of the four Gospel writers as they relate what from any perspective must, if true, have been the most stupendous event ever to occur in human history. The most notable characteristics of Mark's narrative (16:1–8),[14] the earliest, are its remarkable restraint and indirectness. He offers no explanation of how or why the stone was removed.

He only implies, not explicitly states, that the tomb was empty. He does not describe the resurrection itself. It was not witnessed by human beings. If the Gospels were legendary fabrications, we may rest assured that at least one of the evangelists would not have missed the opportunity of depicting the actual resurrection and of adorning the narrative with fantastic features befitting the scene, such as is found in the Gospel of Peter from which you read, Ms. Miller. But that was a *second*-century document with obvious legendary features; the four New Testament Gospels are from the *first* century and are the earliest accounts of the resurrection.

Second, *according to the records, Jesus' appearances after his resurrection were extraordinarily varied, and this points to their authenticity*. We are not confronted in the resurrection narratives with a single appearance of Jesus to one individual or to a group, nor with a single distant sighting of him by one person or by many. The records recount multiple appearances—to individuals, to small groups ranging in size from two to eleven persons, and to at least one larger group. The Christians claimed that he appeared to both men and women, just outside his tomb, on a mountain, in the city, in the country, by a lake, and in an upper room. They further asserted that he appeared for brief and for longer periods, that he appeared in the morning, the afternoon, and the evening, and that he engaged in a variety of activities during his appearances, such as teaching, walking and talking, preparing breakfast, and taking food.

Third, *we have eyewitness testimony that Jesus was seen alive after his resurrection*. It is true that the apostle Paul is the only New Testament writer who, using the first person, says, "He appeared to me also" (1 Cor. 15:8), or asks, "Have I not seen Jesus our Lord?" (1 Cor. 9:1). But we have numerous records of the claims of various Christians that they personally saw Jesus after his resurrection, spoke with him, and ate with him. It would be difficult to overestimate the importance of this testimony. In 1 Corinthians 15:6 Paul refers to some five hundred witnesses, most of whom were still alive at the time of writing in about 55, some twenty-five years after the resurrection. This continuous presence of eyewitnesses in the church for two or more decades after the resurrection served to guarantee the accuracy of the traditions as they became crystallized and widely disseminated and also had the effect of checking any tendency to create or embellish traditions. Hearing a denial of the resurrection or some fanciful story about what Jesus did after he had risen, an eyewitness could easily refute it with the simple assertion "I know; I was there!"

In this regard, the situation of first-century eyewitnesses of the risen Jesus was not unlike that of twentieth-century survivors of the Holocaust. In 1981 a four-day gathering of Jewish survivors of the Nazi concentration camps was held in Jerusalem. About six thousand people from some twenty-three countries joined three thousand Israelis and eight hundred children of survivors in "a celebration of life." Interviewed on television, Ernest Michel, the chairman of the organizing committee and himself a survivor of Auschwitz and Buchenwald, attacked those who suggested that the Holocaust never took place. "These hands have carried off [for burial] more corpses than I care to remember. And some say that the Holocaust never happened! We know; we were there!" What twentieth-century Jewish eyewitnesses say with grief, first-century Jewish eyewitnesses said with joy: "We know; we were there!"

Fourth, *another hint of the Gospels' "ring of truth" is the prominent place accorded to women in the resurrection narratives.* Three women were the first witnesses of the empty tomb (Mark 16:1–4). Two of these women were granted the first angelic appearance and announcement (Matt. 28:5–7; Mark 16:5–7), and Mary Magdalene was given the first appearance of Jesus (John 20:11–17). Among the Jews of that day the testimony of women was not admissible as legal evidence except in a very few particular situations.[15] If all the traditions of Jesus' appearances were merely fabrications, a litany of lies, these special privileges would never have been given to women, but to the apostles as a group, or to an individual such as Peter. So the very existence of these traditions regarding the women confirms their reliability.

Third Speaker for the Affirmative: Eugene Sanderson

A strip of handloomed linen cloth, 14′ 3″ by 3′ 7″, bearing a double image, front and back, of a crucified male Caucasian about 5′ 11″ tall and weighing about 178 pounds. Is it the actual burial shroud of the crucified Jesus—or the world's most spectacular hoax?

Since 1578 the Cathedral of St. John the Baptist in Turin, Italy, has housed this most famous relic of Christendom. To celebrate the four-hundredth anniversary of the shroud's arrival in Turin, there was a rare, six-week public display of the relic in the cathedral, when over 3.3 million people viewed the priceless treasure. As soon as the exhibition closed on October 8, 1978, a team of forty scientists from Europe and the United States began to conduct a comprehensive battery of tests on the shroud for 120 continuous hours, the five days during which they had been permitted to make their investigations. They represented various scientific disciplines, such as chemistry, physics, computer technology, aerodynamics, infrared thermography, biophysics, and forensic pathology.

One unofficial report of the findings of this Shroud of Turin Research Project is found in *Verdict on the Shroud* by K. E. Stevenson and G. R. Habermas. The book's subtitle, *Evidence for the Death and Resurrection of Jesus Christ*, reflects the basic conclusions of the two authors, namely that the shroud is an authentic burial cloth of a first-century Jew, that this Jew was probably none other than Jesus, and that Jesus actually rose from the dead.[16] In an article appearing the same year, Habermas summarized three new arguments for the historicity of the resurrection that he believed were afforded by the shroud.[17] First, whereas other burial shrouds have only blood and decomposition stains, this shroud has a double image (front and back) apparently caused by a burst of light or heat radiation from the dead body. Second, since the shroud contains no evidence of decomposition, the body must not have remained in the cloth "for more than a very few days." Third, the blood clots on the shroud are intact and the dried borders of the blood stains are not disrupted, showing that the body was not removed or unwrapped. Habermas concludes that the shroud's evidence for the resurrection is so strong that "if Jesus was not buried in this garment, then we might have a problem, for it would seem that someone else would have appeared to have risen from the dead."[18]

Let me cite two additional Christian interpretations of the shroud. Listen to Ian Wilson, a BBC radio personality, in his 1978 book on the shroud:

A hypothetical glimpse of the power operating at the moment of creation of the Shroud's image may be ventured. In the darkness of the Jerusalem tomb the dead body of Jesus lay, unwashed, covered in blood, on a stone slab. Suddenly, there is a burst of mysterious power from it. In that instant the blood dematerializes, dissolved perhaps by the flash, while its image and that of the body becomes indelibly fused onto the cloth, preserving for posterity a literal "snapshot" of the Resurrection.

However the image was formed, we may well be entranced by the fourteen-foot length of linen in Turin. For if the author's reconstruction is correct, the Shroud has survived first-century persecution of Christians, repeated Edessan floods, an Edessan earthquake, Byzantine iconoclasm, Moslem invasion, crusader looting, the destruction of the Knights Templars, not to mention the burning incident that caused the triple holes, the 1532 fire, and a serious arson attempt made in 1972. It is ironic that every edifice in which the Shroud was supposedly housed before the fifteenth century has long since vanished through the hazards of time, yet this frail piece of linen has come through almost unscathed.[19]

Then there is Geoffrey Ashe, a British journalist, in his 1966 contribution in *Sindon*, a journal that reports investigation into the shroud and its origins:

The physical change of the body at the resurrection may have released a brief and violent burst of some radiation other than heat—perhaps scientifically identifiable, perhaps not—which scorched the cloth. In this case, the shroud is a quasi-photograph of Christ returning to life, produced by a kind of radiance or "incandescence" partially analogous to heat in its effects. . . . In conclusion, the acceptance of the holy shroud as a "scorch picture"—whatever the precise mode of creation—justifies the following statement: "The shroud is explicable [only] if it once enwrapped a human body to which something extraordinary happened. It is not explicable otherwise."[20]

But all this was prior to 1988.[21] During that year the crucial test that would finally determine the age of the shroud—the carbon-14 test—was carried out. Previously the shroud's custodian, Anastasio Cardinal Ballestrero, had denied permission for this test because it required the removal of handkerchief-sized samples from the shroud. But recent improvements in testing techniques reduced the size of the samples needed to postage-stamp dimensions and the cardinal gave his permission. *Time* magazine reported the testing procedures as follows:

> Testing was done simultaneously at the University of Arizona, Britain's Oxford University and Switzerland's Federal Institute of Technology in Zurich. Each laboratory received four unmarked samples: a shroud cutting and three control pieces, one of which dated from the 1st century. The samples were chemically cleaned, burned to produce carbon dioxide, catalytically converted into graphite and then tested for carbon 14 isotopes to fix the date by calculating the amount of radioactive decay. Only London's British Museum, which coordinated the testing, knew which samples were which.

Once the data from the three institutions had been correlated and averaged, the startling result emerged. There is a 95% probability that the shroud is to be dated between 1260 and 1390 and virtual certainty that it does not predate 1200.

These findings have been acknowledged and accepted by Cardinal Ballestrero and Pope John Paul II.

Exit Habermas, and Wilson, and Ashe, and a host of other Christian hopefuls. How typical of you Christians, grasping for straws and swallowing camels! What a superstitious bunch you are! Your case for the resurrection of Jesus is so weak that it needs to be bolstered up by a linen shroud belonging to the Middle Ages!

Third Speaker for the Negative: Susan Adams

Well, Mr. Sanderson, you certainly had a field day with the shroud! Of course we accept the most recent carbon-14 test results and agree with you that the shroud was not the burial cloth of Jesus and therefore has no relevance for the question of the empty tomb or the resurrection. Yes, some people have perhaps been overzealous in grasping at a straw that might strengthen their case, but that is not because the case needs the straw, but because they are so devoted to the case. Actually, two of the writers you cite, Stevenson and Habermas, give a more cautious evaluation of the data when they write further about the shroud after the tests of 1988.[22] Certainly Christian faith does not rest in a holy relic but in a living person, whose resurrection rests on verifiable facts.

But there does happen to be a piece of archeological data that is relevant. In 1930 a Frenchman, Franz Cumont, published the text of an inscription from Nazareth in Galilee.[23] The inscription is in Greek but is probably a translation of a Latin original. In it the emperor Claudius, who ruled from 41 to 54, decrees the death penalty for anyone violating tombs:

It is my pleasure that sepulchres and tombs, which have been erected as solemn memorials of ancestors or children or relatives, shall remain undisturbed in perpetuity. If it be shown that anyone has either destroyed them or otherwise thrown out the bodies which have been buried there or removed them with malicious intent to another place, thus committing a crime against those buried there, or removed the headstones or other stones, I command that against such person the same sentence be passed in respect of solemn memorials of men as is laid down in respect of the gods. Much rather must one pay respect to those who are buried. Let no one disturb them on any account. Otherwise it is my will that capital sentence be passed upon such person for the crime of tomb-spoliation.[24]

Two questions naturally arise: What prompted an emperor in Rome to give his personal attention to an isolated problem of tomb breaking and body snatching in Galilee (or perhaps more generally in Palestine) and to depart from Roman legal tradition by instituting the death penalty for violation of tombs? And why did Claudius lay down such a severe penalty for only one segment of the empire—significantly, the part to which Jesus had belonged?

We know that in 49 Claudius expelled all Jews (including Jewish Christians) from Rome because of constant rioting, probably in connection with the claims of Christian Jews that Jesus was the Messiah.[25] As a result of the spread of Christianity to Rome, or perhaps in connection with this edict of expulsion, Claudius had made some inquiries about the origin of the Christian movement. Such inquiry would be totally in keeping with what we know of Claudius. He was renowned for his antiquarian interests, and, being eager to carry forward the religious reforms of Augustus, he took an interest in religious issues and problems throughout the Mediterranean. Moreover, Claudius was a close friend of Herod Agrippa I, who had an intimate knowledge of Christian origins and a virulent hatred of Christians (Acts 12:1–5). Evidently Claudius had heard the Jewish claim that the sect of the Nazarenes, which was causing such disturbance in the synagogues of Rome, had been generated by a case of "body snatching," when the disciples of Jesus of Nazareth had broken into his tomb, stolen his body, and then pronounced him to be alive. In this way Claudius may have associated tomb violation with the rise of seditious religious movements. This would have led him to formulate the drastic edict and direct that it be promulgated throughout Galilee or Palestine, or at least in places closely associated with Jesus, such as Nazareth.

I conclude that the Nazareth decree testifies to the wide circulation and influence of the Jewish explanation of the alleged resurrection of Jesus that Matthew 28:13 records: "His disciples came during the night and stole him away." But such an explanation—and Claudius's action that was based on it—presupposes the empty tomb. Both the friends and the adversaries of Jesus agreed that his tomb was empty!

Let me conclude our side's case by drawing your attention to four additional arguments that point to the resurrection of Jesus.

First, only the resurrection adequately explains *the existence and survival of the church.* Any movement's "papers of association" must be taken seriously in seeking to trace its rise. The early Christians traced the origin of their movement to one event, and only one—the resurrection of Christ. That explanation should stand until historical investigation shows it to be inadequate. But it is the other possible explanations that prove inadequate. Neither in Greek philosophy nor in Jewish theology can we find the stimulus for Easter faith. Gentile philosophers scorned the notion of resurrection, while Jewish thought had no precedent for a permanent resurrection from the dead before the Last Day. The doubt of the disciples in the face of the announced resurrection (Luke 24:11) and the persistent skepticism of Thomas (John 20:25) lead us to dismiss the contention that the disciples were gullible fantasizers whose hopes created a resurrected Master. It was not the church that mothered the resurrection; it was the resurrection that mothered the church. C. F. D. Moule, formerly Lady Margaret's Professor of Divinity in the University of Cambridge, puts it this way: "The birth and rapid rise of the Christian Church . . . remain an unsolved enigma for any historian who refuses to take seriously the only explanation offered by the Church itself."[26]

As to the survival of the church, would so improbable a conviction as belief in the resurrection of a crucified Messiah have enabled the church to remain distinct from its parent Judaism unless that belief corresponded to reality?

Second, we should also note *the transformation of the disciples*. Some potent cause must be found to explain the radical conversion of Jesus' disciples from frightened cowards who fled in panic when Jesus was arrested (Mark 14:50) to courageous witnesses who could not be silenced by the Jewish Sanhedrin (Acts 5:17–41). First Corinthians 15:5 suggests the cause: "He appeared to the Twelve." The famous Cambridge classical scholar, T. R. Glover, once remarked:

> Great results have great causes. We have to find, somewhere
> or other, between the crucifixion and the first preaching of
> the disciples in Jerusalem, something that entirely changed
> the character of that group of men. . . . The evidence for
> the Resurrection is not so much what we read in the Gospels
> as what we find in the rest of the New Testament—the new
> life of the disciples.[27]

And how else shall we adequately account for the dramatic
about-face of Saul of Tarsus, at one moment a ruthless
exterminator of Christians (Acts 26:11), but at the next a
champion of the messiahship of Jesus and a tireless pioneer
missionary (Acts 9:1–30), unless it be that the risen Jesus
appeared to him (1 Cor. 15:8)?

Third, some momentous occurrence is needed to explain
*the early Christian change from the Sabbath to Sunday as the prin-
cipal day of worship.* The intensity of Jewish commitment to
the Sabbath may be illustrated by two points. The twenty-
four-hour period from 6:00 P.M. Thursday to 6:00 P.M. Fri-
day was called "the Day of Preparation" (Luke 23:54; John
19:31, 42; cf. Jubilees 2:29), that is, the day when tasks
(including essential tasks such as cooking) were performed
in advance of the Sabbath, so that cessation from labor might
be strictly observed on the holy day. Second, a myriad of
regulations grew up around the Sabbath and formed a
"hedge" around the fourth commandment, protecting people from any possible infringement of this law. At a later
period the Jewish Talmud specified some thirty-nine types
of work that were not permissible on the Sabbath. The
momentous occurrence that triggered the change in the
Christian's day of meeting was nothing other than the resurrection. Sunday was termed "the Lord's Day" (Rev. 1:10)

because it was the day when the Lord Jesus rose and the day when Christians gathered to worship the Lord. So dramatic was the change, so powerful was the resurrection, that Paul, the ardent Pharisee who had been thoroughly trained in every point of Jewish ancestral law (Acts 22:3), could link the weekly Sabbath with annual festivals and monthly new moons as all being "merely a shadow of things that were to come" (Col. 2:16–17).

Finally, we should not overlook *the testimony of Christian believers*. Historically speaking, this has probably induced more conversions to Christ and Christianity than all other evidences of the resurrection combined, for here the resurrection is imprinted for all to see on the living tablets of human lives. Christians claim that Jesus lives because he produces and sustains beneficial change in the whole fabric of their lives—thinking, feeling, willing, and acting.

Summing up for the Affirmative—"That Jesus Christ Did Not Rise from the Dead": Philip Carter

"When I think of the resurrection," H. G. Wells once said, "I am always reminded of the happy endings that editors and actor managers are accustomed to impose on essentially tragic plays and novels." We on the affirmative team believe that the life of Jesus was certainly tragic—here we have a brilliant Jewish rabbi from Galilee, only about thirty-five years old, cut down in the prime of his teaching career, the victim of the religious intrigue of the Jews and the judicial mismanagement of the Romans. The tale of the resurrection was simply a gallant attempt by the Christians to salvage something from what remains one of the greatest tragedies in world history.

But how do we account for the remarkable influence exercised by Jesus for almost twenty centuries? In act 3, scene 1 of Shakespeare's *Julius Caesar*, these words are addressed to Caesar, slumped under the assassin's dagger: "O mighty Caesar! dost thou lie so low? Are all thy conquests, glories, triumphs, spoils, shrunk to this little measure?" But two acts later (act 5, scene 3), there is a further address: "O Julius Caesar, thou art mighty yet! Thy spirit walks abroad." These two quotations apply equally to J. F. Kennedy, whom I mentioned earlier. As he lies slumped in his presidential car under an assassin's bullet: "O mighty Kennedy! dost thou lie so low? Are all thy conquests, glories, triumphs, spoils, shrunk to this little measure?" But Kennedy's spirit lives on—among a host of Democrats, but especially in the Kennedy family: "O John Kennedy, thou art mighty yet! Thy spirit walks abroad." So too in the case of Jesus. As he lies slumped on a Roman cross under a lance thrust: "O mighty Jesus! dost thou lie so low? Are all thy conquests, glories, triumphs, spoils, shrunk to this little measure?" But the personality of Jesus will live for ever. His influence persists among his followers worldwide as they are given to the selfless service of humankind. "O Jesus Christ, thou art mighty yet! Thy spirit walks abroad." Jesus "rose" in the memories of his disciples, in their love, in their service, in their preaching. But as for a bodily resurrection from the tomb—certainly not!

Summing up for the Negative—It Is Not True "That Jesus Christ Did Not Rise from the Dead": Alice Johnson

Can the resurrection of Jesus be "proved"? No more than you can "prove" the existence of God, but rich evidence abounds for both. Evidence is not in itself proof, but it points to some fact or reality. When the fact or reality to which the evidence points is accepted, that evidence becomes "convincing proof." But people can accept and experience the fact that Jesus is alive without ever considering the historical evidence for his resurrection. At the other extreme, however compelling the evidence may be, people who are *unwilling* to accept a certain fact will reject it in spite of the evidence. Imagine, for example, that we were confronted with the original copy of the certificate of Jesus' death written by Pilate. We would remain unconvinced by this conclusive piece of evidence if we wanted to believe that Jesus never existed. So too, even if we had access to an affidavit sworn by the legal consultant of the Sanhedrin or by the president of the society of pathologists in Jerusalem to the effect that Jesus of Nazareth rose from the dead, this evidence would never become a "convincing proof" if we were convinced on other grounds that a dead man could never return to life.

My team contends that an open-minded appraisal of the relevant historical evidence inevitably leads to the conclusions that the grave in which Jesus had been placed was discovered to be empty on the third day after his crucifixion and that Jesus himself appeared to certain persons after his death in a recognizable bodily form.

But, you may well ask, how can an event that occurred almost two thousand years ago affect us today? What is the relevance of this exercise in evaluating historical data? Another irrelevant history lesson?

Past events can have present consequences. The Watergate era has passed, yet it has present significance: American politicians will never be quite the same again—they will not record their conversations on tape when they are tempted to participate in shady deals. But with Jesus it is not just a case of the influence of a past event in the present, the influence of his life and teaching on subsequent generations. It is the claim of the New Testament that the person who rose from the dead two thousand years ago is still alive, in the power of an endless life. The risen Jesus proclaims, "I am the Living One; I was dead, and behold I am alive for ever and ever!" (Rev. 1:18). No one ever claimed that Caesar or Kennedy rose from his grave and is alive for ever! There is something incongruous, if not repulsive, about comparing Jesus Christ with Julius Caesar or John Kennedy. To compare Jesus Christ with mere human beings, however gifted or influential they may have been, is in fact to belittle him. He is unique, in a category of his own, both as a historical figure and as an ever-present person. If Caesar or Kennedy entered the room, we would all immediately stand up. If Jesus came in, we would all instinctively bow down. When the risen Jesus meets us, he comes to us as one who is alive forever, the conqueror of death. He evokes our reverential awe; he prompts our humble worship; he invites our simple belief. The only appropriate response is that of the apostle Thomas, "My Lord and my God!"

Is Jesus God?

My aim in this chapter is straightforward. I wish to summarize the testimony of the New Testament writers concerning the deity of Christ. In chapter 1, I reviewed the evidence of early classical writers that Jesus lived and died in the first century A.D. Chapter 2 was a debate concerning the evidence for the resurrection of Jesus. This extraordinary event suggests that we fail to do full justice to the person of Jesus when we speak only of his manhood. In the present chapter I shall investigate what the New Testament says about this other dimension of Jesus' person, his godhood. It is not my purpose here to discover when a belief in Jesus' deity arose among the early Christians or how it was developed by the various authors of the New Testament. My concern is to synthesize, not analyze; to indicate the overall testimony of the New Testament, not the distinctive contribution of each author.[1]

Is Jesus really God? How can we be sure? How are we sure that a certain person really is, for example, the President of the United States and not an imposter? Basically, in three ways. First, he enjoys a status and prerogatives that are reserved for presidents, such as living in the White House or traveling on Air Force One. Second, he exercises various functions that belong exclusively to the presidency, such as delivering the State of the Union address or assuming the role of Commander-in-Chief. Third, he is addressed as "Mr. President" or referred to as "the President" by his fellow Americans. So also in the case of Jesus. We become sure that he really is God in three ways: if he enjoys a distinctively divine status; if he exercises various functions that belong exclusively to the Godhead; and if he is addressed or referred to as "God." These, then, are the three categories under which I shall consider the New Testament view of the deity of Jesus Christ—*divine status* claimed by or accorded to Jesus, *divine functions* exercised by Jesus, the *divine title* "God" used of Jesus.

I. Divine Status Claimed by or Accorded to Jesus

A. In Relation to God the Father . . .

1. JESUS IS THE POSSESSOR OF DIVINE ATTRIBUTES

One verse beyond all others in the New Testament affirms that every divine attribute is found in Jesus: "In Christ all the fullness of the Deity lives in bodily form" (Col. 2:9). Paul does not say simply "the plenitude of Deity," but "the *entire* fullness of Deity." He emphasizes that no element of that fullness is excepted. Whatever is characteristic of God as God resides in Christ. This includes both God's nature and his attributes. In the Greek text the verb *lives* (present tense) and the adverb translated "in bodily form" are not found side by side but are separated, which suggests that two distinct affirmations are being made: that the entire fullness of the Godhead dwells in Christ eternally and that this fullness now permanently resides in Christ in bodily form. Thus, Paul implies both the eternal deity and the permanent humanity of Christ.

As for specific attributes, certain passages imply that both before and after his earthly life Jesus is omniscient (John 21:17; Acts 1:24), omnipresent (Eph. 4:10), and immutable (Heb. 13:8).[2] What is more, during his earthly life he was sinless and holy (Acts 3:14; 2 Cor. 5:21; Heb. 4:15; 7:26; 1 Pet. 2:22; 1 John 3:5) just as God the Father is holy (Lev. 19:2; Isa. 6:3; 57:15).

2. JESUS IS ETERNALLY EXISTENT

Two verses speak of Christ's existence or activity prior to his incarnation:

Isaiah said this because he saw Jesus' glory and spoke about him. (John 12:41; see Isa. 6:1–3)

They [the Israelites] drank from the spiritual rock that accompanied them, and that rock was Christ. (1 Cor. 10:4)

There are also many passages that speak of the Father's sending of the Son into the world (e.g., John 3:17; Rom. 8:3; Gal. 4:4; 1 John 4:9) or of the Son's coming into the world (e.g., John 1:9; 2 Cor. 8:9) or his appearance on the earthly scene (e.g., Heb. 9:26; 1 Pet. 1:20), all of which presuppose his prior existence.

Other verses affirm Christ's existence prior to creation:

In the beginning was the Word. (John 1:1)

And now, Father, glorify me in your presence with the glory I had with you before the world began. (John 17:5)

But in these last days he [God] has spoken to us by his Son, whom he appointed heir of all things, and through whom he made the universe. (Heb. 1:2)

These three verses imply the eternal preexistence of Jesus but do not explicitly affirm it. The nearest the New Testament comes to affirming this truth in explicit terms is by using the timeless present tense:

> No one has ever seen God, but God the One and Only, who *is* at the Father's side, has made him known. (John 1:18)

> "I tell you the truth," Jesus answered, "before Abraham was born, I *am*!" (John 8:58; cf. Exod. 3:14)

> Who [Christ], *being* in very nature God,
>   did not consider equality with God something to be
>   grasped. (Phil. 2:6)

> He *is* before all things. (Col. 1:17)

> Jesus Christ *is* the same yesterday and today and forever. (Heb. 13:8; the present tense is elided in Greek)

3. JESUS IS EQUAL IN DIGNITY

Nowhere in the Old Testament is the consummate dignity of the God of Israel more extolled than in King David's prayer after he had donated his personal fortune toward the construction of the temple:

> Yours, O LORD, is the greatness and the power
>   and the glory and the majesty and the splendor,
>   for everything in heaven and earth is yours.
> Yours, O LORD, is the kingdom;
>   you are exalted as head over all. (1 Chron. 29:11)

But the New Testament accords to Jesus parity of dignity with the God of Israel. John records the saying of Jesus himself that "the Father judges no one, but has entrusted all judgment to the Son, that all may honor the Son just as they honor the Father. He who does not honor the Son does not honor the Father, who sent him" (John 5:22–23). And so it is that Father and Son are depicted as joint "possessors" of:

a. the divine name: "Baptizing them in the name of the Father and of the Son and of the Holy Spirit" (Matt. 28:19)

b. specific names:

Lord	of God (Exod. 6:2; Isa. 45:5)
	of Jesus (Acts 2:36; 1 Cor. 12:3)
Lord of lords	of God (Deut. 10:17; Ps. 136:3)
	of Jesus (Rev. 17:14; 19:16)
Shepherd	of God (Ps. 23:1; Ezek. 34:11–31)
	of Jesus (John 10:11–16; Heb. 13:20; 1 Pet. 5:4)
Alpha and Omega	of God (Rev. 1:8; 21:6)
	of Jesus (Rev. 22:13; cf. 1:17)

c. the Spirit (Rom. 8:9)
d. the kingdom (Eph. 5:5; Rev. 11:15)
e. the throne (Rev. 22:1, 3)

4. JESUS IS UNIVERSALLY SUPREME

One of the constant refrains found throughout the Old Testament is summed up in the psalmist's words: "You, O

LORD, are the Most High over all the earth; you are exalted
far above all gods" (Ps. 97:9). The early Christians attributed
the same universal supremacy to Jesus. Peter affirms that Jesus
"has gone into heaven and is at God's right hand—with angels,
authorities and powers in submission to him" (1 Pet. 3:22).
Paul states that "Christ died and returned to life so that he
might be the Lord of both the dead and the living" (Rom.
14:9). And John observes that Jesus is "the ruler of the kings
of the earth" (Rev. 1:5). But not only is Jesus supreme over
all heavenly beings and all earthly beings, whether dead or
alive. He stands in authority and rule over the entire universe,
animate and inanimate. He is "over all" (Rom. 9:5) and is
"before all" (Col. 1:17) with regard to both time and status.
In these two verses, the Greek for "all" is ambiguous, for it
may be masculine ("all persons") or neuter ("all things," animate and inanimate). The latter is more probable.

All of these emphases are brought together in Ephesians
1:20–22:

> [God's mighty strength,] which he exerted in Christ when
> he raised him from the dead and seated him at his right hand
> in the heavenly realms, far above all rule and authority, power
> and dominion, and every title that can be given, not only in
> the present age but also in the one to come. And God placed
> all things under his feet and appointed him to be head over
> everything for the church.

5. JESUS IS THE PERFECT REVELATION OF GOD

Central to the Christian tradition is the belief that God
as he is in himself cannot be seen by the physical eye; he is
invisible (1 Tim. 1:17; 1 John 4:12). No one has seen him
or can see him (1 Tim. 6:16). But equally central is the con-

viction that, in Christ, God the Father has revealed himself perfectly. Jesus Christ has accurately and comprehensively made visible the invisible nature of God:

> No one has ever seen God. The only Son, who is God and who resides in the Father's heart—he has revealed him. (John 1:18, my translation)

Only the Son who shares the divine nature (cf. John 1:1) is qualified to reveal the Father personally and completely. John's compound verb (*exēgēsato*, "he has revealed") implies the perfection of God's self-revelation in Christ. In response to Philip's request, "Lord, show us the Father and that will be enough for us" (John 14:8), Jesus remarked, "Anyone who has seen me has seen the Father" (John 14:9).

It is not only the apostle John who expresses this view of the role of Jesus. Paul depicts Jesus as "the image of the invisible God" (Col. 1:15). That is, he is the exact and visible expression of a God who has not been seen and cannot be seen. Then there is the author of Hebrews, who declares that "the Son is the radiance of God's glory and the exact representation of his being" (Heb. 1:3). The two key Greek terms in this verse are colorful. *Apaugasma* ("radiance") pictures Christ as the "outshining" or "effulgence" or "irradiated brightness" of God the Father's inherent glory. *Charaktēr* ("exact representation") points to Christ as the flawless expression of God's nature, one who is indelibly stamped with God's character.

6. JESUS IS THE EMBODIMENT OF TRUTH

Everywhere in the Old Testament the Lord is portrayed as "the God of truth" (e.g., Ps. 31:5; Isa. 65:16). Among other things, this expression implies that his character is upright, his word is dependable, and his actions are consistent.

John and the early church recognized Jesus as "the true light that gives light to every man" (John 1:9), as "the true bread" that "comes down from heaven and gives life to the world" (John 6:32–33), and as "the true vine" that nourishes the branches and produces fruit in them (John 15:1, 4). Moreover, they saw that, because Jesus was God's fully accredited agent (Acts 4:27; 10:38), what he taught about God corresponded to reality and was utterly trustworthy (Matt. 22:16; Luke 20:21; John 8:40, 45). But it is not simply the case that Jesus spoke the truth and that in an absolute sense truth came through him (John 1:17). In two classic affirmations the apostle John declares that Jesus is full of truth (John 1:14) and actually is the truth (John 14:6). He embodies the truth that leads to God and imparts eternal life: "I am the way and the truth and the life" (John 14:6).

B. In Relation to Human Beings . . .

1. JESUS IS THE RECIPIENT OF PRAISE AND WORSHIP

In the first century A.D., religious Jews recited Deuteronomy 6:4 (the *Shema*) twice daily, in the morning and in the evening: "Hear, O Israel: The LORD our God, the LORD is one." This confession of faith affirms that there is only one God—not many—and that he is unique in the universe. But it also implies that God alone is the proper object of worship; to worship the creature rather than the Creator is blasphemy. The first Christians shared this same sense of utter repulsion at the idea that a human being should be worshiped. When the people of Lystra tried to offer sacrifice to Barnabas and Paul, the apostles "tore their clothes and rushed into the crowd, shouting: 'Men, why are you doing this? We too are only men, human like you' " (Acts 14:14–15). Even the worship of angels was repudiated. When the apostle John fell at the feet of an angel in order to worship him, he received the stern rebuke, "Do not do it! . . . Worship God!" (Rev. 19:10).

Against this background we must reckon with two astounding points. First, when he was on earth Jesus received the praise and worship given to him without ever rebuking the persons who acted in this way:

Then those who were in the boat worshiped him, saying, "Truly you are the Son of God." (Matt. 14:33)

But when the chief priests and the teachers of the law saw the wonderful things he did and the children shouting in the temple area, "Hosanna to the Son of David," they were indignant.

"Do you hear what these children are saying?" they asked him.

"Yes," replied Jesus, "have you never read,

'From the lips of children and infants

you have ordained praise'?" (Matt. 21:15–16)

Suddenly Jesus met them [the women]. "Greetings," he said. They came to him, clasped his feet and worshiped him. (Matt. 28:9)

When they [the eleven disciples] saw him, they worshiped him; but some doubted. (Matt. 28:17)

Thomas said to him, "My Lord and my God!" (John 20:28; cf. 5:22–23)

The second remarkable item is that, after Jesus' return to heaven as the exalted Lord, praise and worship of him intensified:

Sing and make music in your heart to the Lord. (Eph. 5:19)

Therefore God exalted him to the highest place
    and gave him the name that is above every name,
that at the name of Jesus every knee should bow,
    in heaven and on earth and under the earth,
and every tongue confess that Jesus Christ is Lord,
    to the glory of God the Father. (Phil. 2:9–11)

And when he [the Lamb] had taken it [the scroll], the four living creatures and the twenty-four elders fell down before the Lamb. . . . And they sang a new song:
    "You are worthy. . . ."
In a loud voice they [many angels] sang:
    "Worthy is the Lamb. . . ."
    Then I heard every creature in heaven and on earth and under the earth and on the sea, and all that is in them, singing:
        "To him who sits on the throne and to the Lamb
        be praise and honor and glory and power, for ever an ever!"
The four living creatures said, "Amen," and the elders fell down and worshiped. (Rev. 5:8–9, 12–14)

Such New Testament passages fully justify the observation of J. R. W. Stott: "Nobody can call himself a Christian who does not worship Jesus. To worship him, if he is not God, is idolatry; to withhold worship from him, if he is, is apostasy."[3]

2. Jesus Is the Addressee in Prayer

All the formal prayers that are recorded in the New Testament are addressed to God the Father.[4] But occasionally prayer was directed to Jesus himself by groups of Christians:

> Then they prayed, "Lord, you know everyone's heart. Show us which of these two you have chosen [cf. 1:2] to take over this apostolic ministry." (Acts 1:24–25)

> To the church of God in Corinth, to those sanctified in Christ Jesus and called to be holy, together with all those everywhere who call on the name of our Lord Jesus Christ— their Lord and ours. (1 Cor. 1:2; cf. Rom. 10:13, citing Joel 2:32)

> If anyone does not love the Lord—a curse be on him. Come, O Lord! (1 Cor. 16:22)

> He who testifies to these things says, "Yes, I am coming soon." Amen. Come, Lord Jesus. (Rev. 22:20)

Moreover, sometimes individual believers addressed Jesus in prayer:

> While they were stoning him, Stephen prayed, "Lord Jesus, receive my spirit." Then he fell on his knees and cried out, "Lord, do not hold this sin against them." (Acts 7:59–60)

> In Damascus there was a disciple named Ananias. The Lord called to him in a vision, "Ananias!"
> "Yes, Lord," he answered. . . .

"Lord," Ananias answered, "I have heard many reports about this man and all the harm he has done to your saints in Jerusalem." (Acts 9:10, 13; cf. 9:15–17)

When I returned to Jerusalem and was praying at the temple, I fell into a trance and saw the Lord speaking. . . .
"Lord," I replied, "these men know that I went from one synagogue to another to imprison and beat those who believe in you." (Acts 22:17–19)

Three times I pleaded with the Lord to take it [a thorn in my flesh] away from me. (2 Cor. 12:8)

Only if the person addressed in prayer was divine would human beings make requests of him for salvation, forgiveness, deliverance from evil, healing, mercy, providential guidance or protection, and security after death.

3. Jesus Is the Object of Saving Faith

One of the recurrent themes of the Old Testament is that "salvation comes from the Lord" (Jon. 2:9); "he alone is . . . my salvation" (Ps. 62:2, 6); "my salvation and my honor depend on God" (Ps. 62:7). When we turn to the New Testament, however, an additional object of saving faith is introduced:

Trust in God; trust also in me [Jesus]. (John 14:1)

All the prophets testify about him [Jesus] that everyone who believes in him receives forgiveness of sins through his name. (Acts 10:43)

Believe in the Lord Jesus, and you will be saved. (Acts 16:31)

For there is no difference between Jew and Gentile—the same Lord [Jesus; see v. 9] is Lord of all and richly blesses all who call on him, for, "Everyone who calls on the name of the Lord will be saved." (Rom. 10:12–13)

In fact, in the New Testament, God himself is relatively infrequently held up as the object of faith (only twelve instances).[5] This is not because Jesus has displaced God the Father as the one we must trust, but because it is in Christ that God meets us in salvation. There are not two competing personal objects of human faith. Only because Jesus is fully divine, intrinsically sharing God's nature and attributes, does he become a legitimate object of trust.

4. JESUS IS THE JOINT SOURCE OF BLESSING

At the beginning of each of Paul's letters is a salutation that ends with a standardized formula: "Grace and peace to you from God our Father and the Lord Jesus Christ" (1 Cor. 1:3 and elsewhere).[6] The apostle is not saying that there are two distinct sources of grace and peace, one divine and one human; significantly, the preposition *from* (in Greek) is not repeated before "the Lord Jesus Christ." Rather, Father and Son jointly form a single source of divine grace and peace. Of no mere human being could it be said that, together with God, he was a fount of spiritual blessing. Only if Paul had regarded Jesus as fully divine could he have spoken this way.

The same theological point is made even more dramatically in two passages within the Thessalonian letters:

Now *may* our God and Father himself and our Lord Jesus *clear the way* for us to come to you. (1 Thess. 3:11)

Here there are two subjects (God and Jesus), yet remarkably the verb ("may . . . clear the way") is singular in Greek. This does not show that Paul equated God with Jesus, as if they were one person, but it does indicate that he assumed the deity of Jesus and so could trace a single action to a single, unified source.

> May our Lord Jesus Christ himself and God our Father, who *loved* us and by his grace *gave* us eternal encouragement and good hope, *encourage* your hearts and *strengthen* you in every good deed and word. (2 Thess. 2:16–17)

All four italicized verbs are singular in Greek, despite being preceded by a double subject. It is just possible that all four verbs refer solely to the Father, but in the light of the close parallel in 1 Thessalonians 3:11 (where the order of the subjects is reversed), it is much more likely that once again Paul is viewing Father and Son as forming virtually a single subject, given the deity of Jesus.

5. JESUS IS THE OBJECT OF DOXOLOGIES

A doxology is a formal ascription of praise, honor, glory, or blessing given to a divine person, but never to a merely human figure. New Testament doxologies are regularly addressed to God,[7] sometimes "through Jesus Christ."[8] But on at least four occasions a doxology is addressed directly to Christ:

> The Lord [Jesus] will rescue me from every evil attack and will bring me safely to his heavenly kingdom. To him be glory for ever and ever. Amen. (2 Tim. 4:18)

> But grow in the grace and knowledge of our Lord and Savior Jesus Christ. To him be glory both now and forever! Amen. (2 Pet. 3:18)

To him who loves us and has freed us from our sins by his blood, and has made us to be a kingdom and priests to serve his God and Father—to him be glory and power for ever and ever! Amen. (Rev. 1:5–6)

Then I heard every creature in heaven and on earth and under the earth and on the sea, and all that is in them singing:
"To him who sits on the throne and to the Lamb
be praise and honor and glory and power, for ever and ever!"
(Rev. 5:13)

All of these New Testament passages leave us in no doubt that the early Christians believed that Jesus of Nazareth had parity of status with the God of Abraham, Isaac, and Jacob. But the idea of status tends to be a static notion. What indications are there in the New Testament that Jesus acted and acts in the same way that God does? What dynamic functions does Jesus perform that show him to be inherently divine?

II. Divine Functions Exercised by Jesus

A. In Relation to the Universe . . .

1. JESUS IS THE CREATOR

Wherever one turns in the Old Testament, God is presented as the one who created the entire universe, animate and inanimate, and the one who constantly sustains what he created. Two psalms well illustrate God's dual role as Creator and Sustainer of all:

In the beginning you laid the foundations of the earth,
and the heavens are the work of your hands. (Ps. 102:25)

> How many are your works, O LORD!
>> In wisdom you made them all;
>> the earth is full of your creatures. . . .
> These all look to you
>> to give them their food at the proper time. . . .
> When you send your Spirit,
>> they are created,
>> and you renew the face of the earth. (Ps. 104:24, 27, 30)

This emphasis on God's work in creating and sustaining the universe is maintained in the New Testament (Acts 17:24–25, 28; Rom. 11:36; Heb. 2:10).

In the prologue to the Fourth Gospel, however, John states that "through him [the eternal Word] all things were made; without him nothing was made that has been made" (John 1:3). Here the Greek for "all things" (*panta*) draws attention to the multiplicity and diversity of creation. In Colossians 1:16, on the other hand, the Greek for "all things" (*ta panta*) means "all things collectively," with the emphasis being on the sum total of reality: "For in him all things in heaven and on earth were created, things visible and things invisible, whether thrones or dominions or principalities or powers—all things have been created through him and for him" (my translation). Two other points in this remarkable verse are worthy of note. The prepositional phrase *in him* indicates that in the very person of Christ resides the creative energy that produced the universe. John simply says that "in him was life" (John 1:4), while Peter refers to him as "the author of life" (Acts 3:15). The other notable feature is the subtle distinction, lost in many English translations, that Paul makes between the two tenses of creation (*ektisthē . . . ektistai*). A paraphrase of the verse will highlight the distinction:

> It was in his person that all things in heaven and on earth *were once created*, things that can be seen by the human eye, and those things that cannot be seen, whether they be the angelic occupants of heavenly thrones or supernatural beings who exercise dominion or rule or authority—all these things *were created, and now exist*, through him and for him.

The universe has an ongoing relationship to Christ, which leads directly to the next point.

2. JESUS IS THE SUSTAINER

Not only does the universe owe its existence to Jesus Christ; it also owes its coherence to him. "In him," says Paul, "all things hold together" (Col. 1:17). What Christ once created he now maintains in permanent order, stability, and productivity. He is the source of the unity and cohesiveness of the whole universe. This dual theme of creation and its maintenance is found in Hebrews 1, as well as in Colossians 1:

> [God's Son], whom he [God] appointed heir of all things, and through whom he made the universe. The Son is the radiance of God's glory and the exact representation of his being, sustaining all things by his powerful word. (Heb. 1:2–3)

By the same mighty word that brought the universe into existence, Jesus continues to uphold and direct the entire created order.

B. In Relation to Human Beings . . .

1. JESUS TAUGHT AND HEALED WITH AUTHORITY

Twice in Matthew's Gospel it is said that Jesus went throughout the towns and villages of Galilee "teaching in their synagogues, preaching the good news of the kingdom and healing every disease and sickness" (Matt. 4:23; 9:35). These two verses are carefully placed within this Gospel, for they encase (by the literary device called *inclusio*) a classic instance of Jesus' teaching in the Sermon on the Mount (chaps. 5–7) and illustrative examples of Jesus' healing (chaps. 8–9). Now it is true that the twelve disciples of Jesus were in turn directed to "heal every disease and sickness" (Matt. 10:1) and to teach (Matt. 28:20), but the crucial difference between them and Jesus is that they received their authorization and power to act in these ways from Jesus himself. As in the case of the crippled beggar at the temple gate in Jerusalem, the apostolic power to heal derived from Jesus. "Peter said, 'Silver or gold I do not have, but what I have I give you. In the name of Jesus Christ of Nazareth, walk' " (Acts 3:6; cf. 4:10). So also at Lydda, where Peter addressed the bed-ridden paralytic Aeneas with the words "Jesus Christ heals you. Get up and take care of your mat" (Acts 9:34). The same applies to the teaching activity of the apostles. It gained its potency from two facts: they were commissioned to teach by Jesus, to whom "all authority in heaven and on earth" had been given (Matt. 28:18), and they were instructed to teach Jesus' disciples in all nations to obey everything he had commanded them (Matt. 28:20), namely, "the good news of the kingdom" that centered on him and his sacrificial death. The message was potent because of its source and because of its content.

Not surprisingly, the contemporaries of Jesus were astonished at his teaching and his healing, for they unerringly recognized that repeated instantaneous cures and personally authoritative teaching pointed to a healer and teacher who was more than human:[9] "The people were amazed at his teaching, because he taught them as one who had authority, not as the teachers of the law" (Mark 1:22; cf. Matt. 7:28). Whereas the duly licensed rabbis of the day expounded the traditions they had inherited, this Galilean teacher gave his teaching on the authority of his own person as "the Holy One of God" (Mark 1:24). As he himself later expressed it, "Heaven and earth will pass away, but my words will never pass away" (Mark 13:31). Amazement also marked the reaction of onlookers when Jesus performed a healing. After Jesus had commanded the paralytic at Capernaum to get up, "immediately he stood up in front of them, took what he had been lying on and went home praising God. Everyone was amazed and gave praise to God. They were filled with awe and said, 'We have seen remarkable things today' " (Luke 5:25–26). Matthew notes that the crowd was "filled with awe; and they praised God, who had given such authority to men" (Matt. 9:8).

2. JESUS DISPENSED THE SPIRIT

According to Old Testament thought, the new Age would be marked by God's giving of his Spirit, who would be poured out on humankind like revitalizing rain:

And afterward,
   I will pour out my Spirit on all people.
Your sons and daughters will prophesy,
   your old men will dream dreams,

> your young men will see visions.
> Even on my servants, both men and women,
> I will pour out my Spirit in those days. (Joel 2:28–29)

Peter recognized that this prophecy of Joel was fulfilled at Pentecost, for he cites this passage at the beginning of his sermon on the day of Pentecost, substituting "in the last days" for Joel's "and afterward," and also adding "God declares." It is therefore unambiguous that the bestowal of the Spirit is an exclusively divine function. Yet in the same sermon Peter later explains that it was none other than Jesus, raised to life and exalted to the right hand of God, who had received the promised Holy Spirit from the Father and had poured him out (Acts 2:32–33). Such action on the part of Jesus also fulfilled John the Baptist's prophecy about his successor: "He will baptize you with the Holy Spirit" (Matt. 3:11).

3. Jesus Raises the Dead

The Old Testament makes it clear that the ability to raise persons from death rests with God alone. Whether resurrection from the dead involved simply the renewal of mortal life on earth or both reanimation and transformation leading to eternal life in heaven, it was the work of God: "The LORD brings death and makes alive; he brings down to the grave and raises up" (1 Sam. 2:6).

The four Gospels record three cases in which Jesus restored persons to physical life: the son of the widow of Nain (Luke 7:11–17), the daughter of Jairus (Mark 5:21–24, 35–43),[10] and Lazarus (John 11:1–44).[11] But the New Testament also assigns Jesus a distinctive role in the resurrection on the Last Day:

For just as the Father raises the dead and gives them life, even so the Son gives life to whom he is pleased to give it. . . .

A time is coming when all who are in their graves will hear his [the Son's] voice and come out—those who have done good will rise to live and those who have done evil will rise to be condemned. (John 5:21, 28–29)

And in John's next chapter we find the recurring refrain in reference to Jesus and the person who believes in him: "I will raise him up at the last day" (John 6:40; cf. 6:39, 44, 54).

4. Jesus Forgives Sins

Never did the opponents of Jesus more accurately reflect biblical teaching than when they asked, "Who can forgive sins but God alone?" (Mark 2:7). Their sharp retort was occasioned by Jesus' word to the paralyzed man at Capernaum: "Son, your sins are forgiven" (Mark 2:5). Jesus was not offering forgiveness to someone who had wronged him. Nor was he merely announcing that the man's sins had been forgiven by God. He was proclaiming his own "authority on earth to forgive sins" (Mark 2:10). The answer to the question "Who is able to forgive sins besides the One God in heaven?" is "the Son of Man on earth." In a similar episode, Jesus says to a woman of ill repute, "Your sins are forgiven." Luke immediately notes that the guests in the house of Simon the Pharisee "began to say among themselves, 'Who is this who even forgives sins?' " (Luke 7:48–49).

After Jesus' return to heaven, he did not forfeit the exercise of this divine prerogative. Peter declared to the Jewish Sanhedrin in Jerusalem that "God exalted him [Jesus] to his own right hand as Prince and Savior that he might give repentance and forgiveness of sins to Israel" (Acts 5:31).

And Paul encouraged the Colossians, "Forgive as the Lord [Jesus] forgave you" (Col. 3:13).

5. JESUS GRANTS SALVATION OR ETERNAL LIFE

From the beginning to the end of the Old Testament, the Lord God is portrayed as the sole source of physical and spiritual salvation. Said the psalmist, "He alone is my rock and my salvation" (Ps. 62:2, 6), "the Rock of our salvation" (Ps. 95:1). Salvation, which "comes from the Lord" (Jon. 2:9), "will last forever" (Isa. 51:6).

New Testament writers trace the benefits of the new covenant to Jesus as well as to God. Perhaps this is most clearly seen in each of the three chapters of Titus, where exactly the same expression, "our Savior," is applied first to God (Titus 1:3; 2:10; 3:4) and then almost immediately to Jesus (Titus 1:4; 2:13; 3:6). Correspondingly, the author of Hebrews can affirm that after Jesus had fulfilled his ministry of suffering "he became the source of eternal salvation for all who obey him" (Heb. 5:9). It is God the Father who has rescued believers from the dominion of darkness (Col. 1:13), yet it is Jesus the Son who will rescue them from the coming wrath (1 Thess. 1:10). Within the Johannine corpus, eternal life is seen as a gift that God gives (1 John 5:11) or that Jesus Christ grants (John 10:28; 17:2). And we have already seen that at the beginning of his letters Paul describes "grace and peace" as emanating jointly from God the Father and Jesus.

6. JESUS EXERCISES JUDGMENT

Written large across both Testaments are assertions such as "judgment belongs to God" (Deut. 1:17), "the LORD . . . will bring judgment on all mankind" (Jer. 25:31), and "we will all stand before God's judgment seat" (Rom.

14:10). The new element introduced by the New Testament writers is that God will judge all human beings through his Son. In his conversation with Cornelius at Caesarea, Peter observes that Jesus "is the one whom God appointed as judge of the living and the dead" (Acts 10:42). During his speech before the council of the Areopagus in Athens, Paul affirms that God "has set a day when he will judge the world with justice by the man he has appointed" (Acts 17:31). Paul can therefore speak of both the judgment seat of God (Rom. 14:10) and the judgment seat of Christ (2 Cor. 5:10), depicting not two distinct judgments, but one—that of God through Christ. The apostle John expresses the point still more boldly: "The Father judges no one, but has entrusted all judgment to the Son, that all may honor the Son just as they honor the Father" (John 5:22–23). As God's agent, Jesus will judge all persons (Matt. 7:22–23; 16:27) and those on whom he passes a verdict of condemnation will be eternally shut out from his presence (2 Thess. 1:8–9; cf. Matt. 7:23; 25:41).

C. Jesus and Yahweh

Yahweh is the Hebrew name of the God of Israel. Sometimes it is written in the artificial form "Jehovah,"[12] but in English translations it has traditionally been rendered by LORD, written in small capital letters.

Thus far in this chapter I have shown that the New Testament writers credit Jesus with a status that the Old Testament reserves for God and describe him as exercising functions that lie exclusively within the divine domain. This correlation between the status and roles of Jesus and the status and roles of God is further confirmed by certain Old

Testament passages that in their original setting refer exclusively to Yahweh but that are applied to Jesus in the New Testament with what H. R. Mackintosh calls "unembarrassed simplicity."[13] So that this correspondence between the Testaments may be clearly visible, it will be helpful to set out the passages in two columns.

1. THE CHARACTER OF YAHWEH.

God said to Moses, "I AM WHO I AM. This is what you are to say to the Israelites: 'I AM has sent me to you.' "   (Exod. 3:14)

"I tell you the truth," Jesus answered, "before Abraham was born, I am!"   (John 8:58)

This is what the LORD says—
  Israel's King and Redeemer,
    the LORD Almighty:
I am the first and I am the last;
  apart from me there is no God.
                (Isa. 44:6)

When I saw him [Jesus], I fell at his feet as though dead. Then he placed his right hand on me and said: "Do not be afraid. I am the First and the Last."   (Rev. 1:17)

They [the heavens and earth] will
    perish, but you [my God]
    remain;
  they will all wear out like a
    garment.
You will change them like a robe,
  and they will be discarded.

But you remain the same,
  and your years will never end.
    (Ps. 102:26–27, Septuagint)

They [the heavens and earth] will
    perish, but you [the Son]
    remain;
  they will all wear out like a
    garment.
You will roll them up like a robe;
  like a garment they will be
    changed.
But you remain the same,
  and your years will never end.
                (Heb. 1:11–12)

So this is what the Sovereign
    LORD says:
"See, I lay a stone in Zion,
  a tested stone,
a precious cornerstone for a sure
    foundation;

the one who trusts (in him [Septuagint]) will never be dismayed. (Isa. 28:16)	the one/anyone who trusts in him [Jesus the Lord] will never be put to shame (Rom. 9:33; 10:11; 1 Pet. 2:6)

2. THE HOLINESS OF YAHWEH

Do not fear what they fear, and do not dread it. The LORD Almighty is the one you are to regard as holy. (Isa. 8:12–13)	"Do not fear what they fear; do not be frightened." But in your hearts set apart Christ as Lord. (1 Pet. 3:14–15)

3. THE WORSHIP OF YAHWEH

By myself I [the LORD] have
    sworn,
  my mouth has uttered in all
    integrity
a word that will not be revoked:

Before me every knee will bow; by me every tongue will swear. (Isa. 45:23)	That at the name of Jesus every knee should bow, in heaven and on earth and under the earth, and every tongue confess that Jesus Christ is Lord. (Phil. 2:10–11)

Let all God's angels worship
  him [the Lord].
      (Deut. 32:43, Septuagint)

Worship him [the Lord],
  all you his angels.
      (Ps. 97:7, Septuagint)

And again, when God brings his
firstborn into the world, he says,
"Let all God's angels worship
  him."   (Heb. 1:6)

4. THE CREATION WORK OF YAHWEH

In the beginning, O Lord [God],
  you laid the foundations of
  the earth,
and the heavens are the work of
  your hands.
      (Ps. 102:25, Septuagint)

In the beginning, O Lord [Jesus],
  you laid the foundations of
  the earth,
and the heavens are the work of
  your hands.   (Heb. 1:10)

5. THE SALVATION OF YAHWEH

For there is no difference between
Jew and Gentile—the same Lord
[Jesus] is Lord of all and richly
blesses all who call on him, for,
"Everyone who calls on the name
of the Lord will be saved."
      (Rom. 10:12–13 [Acts 2:21])

And everyone who calls
  on the name of the LORD will
    be saved.   (Joel 2:32)

This is he [John the Baptist] who
was spoken of through the
prophet Isaiah:
"A voice of one calling in the
desert,
'Prepare the way for the Lord
    [Jesus the Messiah],
  make straight paths for him.'"
                          (Matt. 3:3)

A voice of one calling:
"In the desert prepare
  the way for the LORD;
make straight in the wilderness
  a highway for our God."
                      (Isa. 40:3)

6. THE JUDGMENT OF YAHWEH

And he [the LORD Almighty] will
   be a sanctuary;
  but for both houses of Israel
    he will be
a stone that causes men to stumble
   and a rock that makes them fall.
              (Isa. 8:14)

A stone [Jesus Christ] that causes
   men to stumble
  and a rock that makes them fall.
    (1 Pet. 2:8 [Rom. 9:33])

7. THE TRIUMPH OF YAHWEH

When you [the LORD God]
   ascended on high,
  you led captives in your train;
  you received gifts from men.
         (Ps. 68:18)

This is why it says:
  "When he [Christ] ascended on
   high,
  he led captives in his train and
  gave gifts to men."   (Eph. 4:8)

If, then, several Old Testament passages referring to Yahweh are directly applied to Jesus by New Testament writers, what are we to deduce about the relation of Jesus to Yahweh? Christians have given two answers to this question. Some make a straight personal equation, "Jesus is Yahweh." This assumes that Yahweh is a personal name that may be appropriately applied to both God the Father and Jesus. "The name . . . above every name" that God gave to Jesus at the resurrection (Phil. 2:9–11) was the name *Kyrios* ("Lord"), which in the Greek Old Testament represents the personal name of the God of Israel, Yahweh. Others argue that although Jesus shares the status and roles of Yahweh, he remains personally distinct from Yahweh. This assumes that Yahweh is a personal name that refers to the Father alone, so that the New Testament distinction between

Father and Son corresponds exactly to the distinction between Yahweh and Jesus. On either view, Jesus' parity of status and function with Yahweh points to their identity of nature.[14] It is precisely this identity of nature that is highlighted by the New Testament passages where Jesus is actually given the divine title *God*. To a discussion of these passages we now turn.

III. The Divine Title "God" Used of Jesus

The New Testament is replete with titles of Jesus, descriptive terms that indicate his status, character, or function.[15] But only one of these titles explicitly describes his character or nature—the Greek term *theos* ("God"). There are at least seven New Testament passages where Jesus is called "God."[16]

John 1:1

In the beginning was the Word, and the Word was with God, and the Word was God.

The first verse of the Prologue (1:1–18) to the Fourth Gospel is clearly triadic: each of the three clauses has the same subject ("the Word") and an identical verb ("was"; Greek *ēn*). The Greek term translated "Word" is *logos*, which includes the idea of reason as well as speech, so that, as one commentator puts it, "Christ is declared by the Apostle to be the Inward and Expressed Thought of the Eternal Mind."[17] Although Jesus Christ is not explicitly mentioned until verse 17, the evangelist clearly assumes that the *Logos* is none other than Jesus Christ, the "only Son" (John 1:14, 18).

The verse makes three separate affirmations about the Word: he already existed when creation and time began (v. 1a); he was always in active communion with God the Father (v. 1b); he was always a partaker of deity (v. 1c). The thought of the verse moves from eternal preexistence to personal intercommunion to intrinsic deity. In the third clause, "the Word was God," the word *theos* ("God") lacks the Greek definite article, which in this case indicates three things: that "God" is predicative, not the subject; that the proposition is nonreciprocating, so that while it is true that "the Word was God," it is not true that God in his totality was the Word; that the term *theos* describes the nature of the Logos rather than identifying his person. Jesus as the Logos is personally distinct from the Father (v. 1b) yet is one with the Father in nature (v. 1c).

John 1:18

No one has ever seen God. The only Son, who is God and who resides in the Father's heart—he has revealed him. (my translation)

There is an important textual variant in John 1:18. Instead of reading *monogenēs theos* ("the only Son, God"), many manuscripts read *ho monogenēs huios* ("the only Son"). But the majority of text critics agree that *monogenēs theos* was the original reading. Some English translations render this phrase by "the only begotten God" (New American Standard Bible) or "God the only Son" (New International Version, New Revised Standard Version). The use of *monogenēs* elsewhere in the New Testament and the word order of the Greek suggest that we should follow the lead of the New American Bible (second edition) and several commentators and translate the phrase by "the only Son, God," where the word *God* explains who "the only Son" is. This is how I arrived at the rendering preferred above—"the only Son,

who is God." John's point in the verse is that, although no
person on earth can claim to have gained knowledge of God
as he is in himself, Jesus Christ, the only Son, has accurately
and fully revealed God to humankind, since he himself is
God by nature and intimately acquainted with the Father
by experience.

John 20:28

Thomas answered and said to him, "My Lord and my God!"
(New American Bible, second edition)

On occasion Thomas's statement has been interpreted as
an exclamation that expresses his praise to God for the miracle of the resurrection of Jesus: "Praise be to my Lord and
my God!" Fatal to this interpretation is the phrase *said to
him* (i.e., Jesus) (*eipen autō*), which is clearly parallel to the
surrounding verses: "He [Jesus] said to Thomas" (v. 27) and
"Jesus said to him [Thomas]" (v. 29). What we have in verse
28 is not an ejaculation made in the hearing of Jesus but an
exclamation actually addressed to him. In effect Thomas is
saying, "You are my Lord and my God." He recognized that
Jesus, now alive from the dead, was supreme over all physical and spiritual life ("Lord") and one who shared the divine
nature ("God").

Was Thomas's cry an extravagant acclamation, spoken in
a moment of ecstasy when his exuberance outstripped his
theological sense? Not at all. John records no rebuke of Jesus
to Thomas for his worship. Jesus' silence is tantamount to
consent, for Jews regarded the human acceptance of worship as blasphemous. Indeed, Jesus' subsequent word to
Thomas, "you have believed" (v. 29a), implies that he

accepted Thomas's confession of faith, which he then indi-
rectly commends to others (v. 29b). Moreover, John himself has endorsed Thomas's confession, for it stands as his
last and highest affirmation about Christ immediately before
his statement of purpose in writing the Gospel (vv. 30–31).

Romans 9:5

To them [the Israelites] belong the patriarchs, and from
them, according to the flesh, comes the Messiah, who is
over all, God blessed forever. Amen. (New Revised Standard
Version)

In the first five verses of Romans 9, Paul is expressing his
sorrow and anguish at the failure of the majority of his fellow Jews to embrace the salvation found in Christ. To explain
why his grief was so intense, Paul lists the incomparable
privileges that belonged to the Jews, the consummate priv-
ilege being that "from their ranks came the Messiah as far
as human descent is concerned" (v. 5a, my translation). At
this point in the verse some editors of the Greek text and
some translations put a semicolon or period, which has the
effect of making the last part of the verse a doxology
addressed to God the Father: "God who is over all be blessed
for ever. Amen" (Revised Standard Version). However, considerations of the word order in Greek make it much more
natural to regard the final words of the verse as a description of or doxology to the Messiah, Jesus Christ (as in the
New Revised Standard Version cited above). What the apostle Paul is affirming at the end of Romans 9:1–5 is this.
Despite the fact that most of his fellow Jews have rejected
their Messiah, Jesus Christ is in reality supreme over the
whole universe, animate and inanimate, and, what is more,

as God by nature, he is and always will be the object of worship.

There has recently been a stunning reversal of scholarly opinion about this verse, a verse that is crucial in any consideration of Paul's view of Christ. In the two standard texts of the Greek New Testament (the Nestle-Aland text, now in its twenty-sixth edition, and the United Bible Societies text, now in its fourth edition), the editors have reversed their earlier punctuation that made verse 5b a doxology to God and now prefer the punctuation that makes verse 5b a description of or doxology to Christ ("the Messiah, who is over all, God blessed forever"; or, "the Messiah, who is God over all, blessed forever"). This remarkable change of interpretation is reflected in the New Revised Standard Version cited above.

Titus 2:13 and 2 Peter 1:1

While we wait for the blessed hope—the glorious appearing of our great God and Savior, Jesus Christ.

To those who through the righteousness of our God and Savior Jesus Christ have received a faith as precious as ours.

Titus 2:13 and 2 Peter 1:1 may be considered together, since both use a stereotyped formula, "God and Savior," in reference to Jesus. This was a common formula in first-century religious terminology, used by both Palestinian and Diaspora Jews in reference to Yahweh, the one true God, and by Gentiles when they spoke of an individual god or a deified ruler. In all of these uses the expression *God and Savior* invariably denotes one deity, not two, so that when Paul and Peter employ this formula and follow it with the name *Jesus Christ*, their readers would always understand it as referring to a single person, Jesus Christ. It would simply not occur to them that "God" might mean the Father, with Jesus Christ as the "Savior."

Hebrews 1:8a

But to the Son he [God] says:
> Your throne, God, is for ever and ever. (New Jerusalem Bible)

Hebrews 1:8 is a quotation of Psalm 45:6, where, at his wedding, a king of David's line is exuberantly addressed as "God" because he represented God to his people and because he foreshadowed the coming royal Messiah, who would perfectly realize the dynastic ideal as described in the psalm. In the first two chapters of Hebrews the author is demonstrating the superiority of Jesus over angels, first as the Son of God (1:5–14), then as the Son of Man (2:5–18). The contrast between 1:7 and 1:8 is not only between the transient service of angels and the permanent dominion of the Son but also between the impermanence of angelic form and the divinity of the Son's person. They are at one time "winds," at another, "flames of fire" (1:7), whereas his person is divine. Only one who fully possesses the divine nature could be appropriately addressed as "God" by God the Father. The superiority of Jesus to angels does not reside simply in his having distinctive titles, such as "Son" (1:5) or "firstborn" (1:6a), in his being the object of angelic worship (1:6b), or in his being the unchangeable Lord of creation (1:10–12) and God's exalted co-regent (1:13). It is also seen in his belonging to a different category of being—that of deity. The address *O God* that was figurative and hyperbolic when applied to a mortal king in Psalm 45 is applied to the immortal Son in a literal and true sense in Hebrews 1.

General Observations

This brings to an end our brief survey of these seven crucial passages. Seen as a whole, they prompt some general observations. First, the ascription of the title *God* to Jesus is found in four New Testament writers—John (three uses), Paul (two), Peter (one), and the author of Hebrews (one). Second, this christological use of the title began immediately after the resurrection in 30 (John 20:28), continued during the 50s (Rom. 9:5) and 60s (Titus 2:13; Heb. 1:8; 2 Pet. 1:1), and then into the 90s (John 1:1, 18). Third, the use of "God" in reference to Jesus was not restricted to Christians who lived in one geographical region or who had a particular theological outlook. It occurs in literature that was written in Asia Minor (John, Titus), Greece (Romans), and possibly Judea (Hebrews) and Rome (2 Peter), and that was addressed to persons living in Asia Minor (John, 2 Peter), Rome (Romans, Hebrews), and Crete (Titus). Also, the use is found in a theological setting that is Jewish Christian (John, Hebrews, Peter) or Gentile Christian (Romans, Titus). Fourth, the three instances in John's Gospel are strategically placed. This Fourth Gospel begins (1:1) as it ends (20:28), and the Prologue to this Gospel begins (1:1) as it ends (1:18), with an unambiguous assertion of the deity of Christ: "The Word was God" (1:1); "the only Son, who is God" (1:18); "my Lord and my God!" (20:28).[18] In his preincarnate state (1:1), in his incarnate state (1:18), and in his postresurrection state (20:28), Jesus is God. For John, recognition of Christ's deity is the hallmark of the Christian.

But, you may ask, why are there so few examples of this usage in the New Testament? If Jesus really is God, why is he not called "God" more often? After all, there are over 1,300 uses of the Greek word *theos* in the New Testament. Several reasons may be given to explain this apparently strange usage.

First, in all strands of the New Testament the term *theos* usually refers to the Father. We often find the expression *God the Father*, which implies that God is the Father.[19] Also, in trinitarian formulas "God" always denotes the Father, never the Son or the Spirit. For example, 2 Corinthians 13:14 reads, "May the grace of the Lord Jesus Christ, and the love of God, and the fellowship of the Holy Spirit be with you all." What is more, in the salutations at the beginning of many New Testament letters, "God" is distinguished from "the Lord Jesus Christ." So Paul's letters regularly begin, "Grace and peace to you from God our Father and the Lord Jesus Christ." As a result of all this, in the New Testament the term *theos* in the singular has become virtually a proper name, referring to the trinitarian Father.[20] If Christ were everywhere called "God," so that in reference to him the term was not a title but a proper noun, like "Jesus," linguistic ambiguity would be everywhere present. What would we be able to make of a statement such as "God was in God, reconciling the world to himself," or "the Father was in God, reconciling the world to himself" (cf. 2 Cor. 5:19)?

Second, another reason why "God" regularly denotes the Father and rarely the Son is that such usage is suited to protect the personal distinction between Son and Father, which is preserved everywhere in the New Testament. Nowhere is this distinction more evident than where the Father is called "the God of our Lord Jesus Christ" (Eph. 1:17) or "his God and Father" (Rev. 1:6), and where Jesus speaks of "my God."[21]

Closely related to this second reason is a third. The New Testament clearly indicates that Jesus is subordinate to God. Although they both possess the divine nature, there is an order in their operation. It is the role of the Father to direct, of the Son to obey. Theologians refer to a functional subordination alongside an essential equality. Consequently, Christ can be said to belong to God (1 Cor. 3:23) and to be subjected to God (1 Cor. 15:28). So, then, by customarily reserving the term *theos* for the Father, New Testament writers were highlighting the Son's subordination to the Father, but not the Father's subordination to the Son. We often find the expression *Son of God* where God is the Father, but never *Father of God* where God is the Son.

Fourth, if Jesus had been regularly called "God" by the early Christians, problems would have been created for their evangelistic efforts. Their Jewish friends would have been convinced that Christians had given up monotheism, for there were now two "Gods": Yahweh and Jesus. On the other hand, their Gentile neighbors would have viewed Jesus as simply another deity to be added to their roster of gods.

Finally, the New Testament authors generally reserve the term *theos* for the Father in order to safeguard the real humanity of Jesus. If "God" had become a personal name for Christ, interchangeable with "Jesus," the humanity of Jesus would tend to be eclipsed; he would seem to be an unreal human being, a divine visitor merely masquerading as a man.

Conclusions

If, then, the word *God* does not become a personal name for Jesus anywhere in the New Testament, what is the actual significance of the seven uses? As used of Jesus, the term *theos* is a generic title, a description that indicates the class or category (*genus*) to which he belongs. Jesus is not only God in revelation, the revealer of God (an official title)— he is God in essence. Not only are the deeds and words of Jesus the deeds and words of God—the nature of Jesus is the nature of God. By nature, as well as by action, Jesus is God. Other New Testament titles of Jesus, such as "Son of God" or "Lord" or "Alpha and Omega," imply the divinity of Jesus, but the title *God* explicitly affirms his deity.

It may help to illustrate the distinction I am making between a proper noun (in this case, a personal name), a generic title, and an official title. Consider these two sentences: Winston Churchill was a Britisher and a prime minister of the United Kingdom. John Kennedy was an American and a president of the United States. In these sentences "Winston Churchill" and "John Kennedy" are proper nouns (personal names); "Britisher" and "American" are generic titles; "prime minister" and "president" are official titles. The parallel sentence relevant to our discussion would be "Jesus is God and the Revealer of God."

Can we, therefore, claim that the New Testament teaches that Jesus is "God"? Yes indeed, provided we constantly bear in mind several factors.

First, to say that "Jesus is God" is true to New Testament thought, but it goes beyond actual New Testament diction. The nearest comparable statements are "the Word was God" (John 1:1), "the only Son, who is God" (John 1:18), and "the Messiah, who is over all, God blessed forever" (Rom. 9:5). So we must remember that the theological proposition "Jesus is God" is an inference from the New Testament evidence—a necessary and true inference, but nonetheless an inference.

Second, if we make the statement "Jesus is God" without qualification, we are in danger of failing to do justice to the whole truth about Jesus—that he was the incarnate Word, a human being, and that in his present existence in heaven he retains his humanity, although now it is in a glorified form. Jesus is not simply "man" nor only "God," but the God-man.

Third, given English usage of the word *God*, the simple affirmation "Jesus is God" may be easily misinterpreted. In common English usage *God* is a proper name, identifying a particular person, not a common noun designating a class.[22] For us *God* is the God of the Judeo-Christian monotheistic tradition, or God the Father of Jesus and of the Christian, or the trinitarian Godhead. So when we make the equation in English, "Jesus is God," we are in danger of suggesting that these two terms, "Jesus" and "God," are interchangeable, that there is a numerical identity between the two. But while Jesus is God, it is not true that God is Jesus. There are others—the Father and the Spirit—of whom the predicate *God* may be rightfully used. Jesus is all that God is, without being all there is of God. The person of Jesus does not exhaust the category of deity. So then, when we say, "Jesus is God," we must recognize that we are attaching a meaning to the term *God*—namely, "God in essence" or "God by nature"— that is not its predominant sense in English.

My analysis of the New Testament evidence for the deity of Christ is now complete. The three branches of evidence we have examined all point in the same direction. Whether we consider the status Jesus enjoys, the functions he performs, or the title he bears, there can be no doubt that the early Christians believed in his full divinity as an essential ingredient of their teaching. Consequently, any modern form of Christianity that has surrendered a wholehearted belief in Jesus' deity has drifted from its moorings and is at sea in a vessel that has forfeited its rating as "Christian." On the other hand, when we bow the knee before the risen Jesus and make the confession of Thomas our own, we are securely moored to uniform Christian tradition and, more importantly, to the divine Person who is at the center of that tradition. Can you—will you—address Jesus with the words "My Lord and my God"?

Epilogue

I have answered each of the three questions with a resounding "Yes!" Yet there is one sense in which each question might also be answered by a "Yes, but. . . ."

Yes, Jesus really existed, *but* he also preexisted, in that he existed in heaven prior to his entering the human scene. Jesus himself expressed it in a linguistic paradox: "Before Abraham was born, I am!" (John 8:58). There was no time when he did not exist with his Father in heaven.

Yes, Jesus really rose from the dead, *but* he never will face death again. This is the way Paul puts it: "Since Christ was raised from the dead, he cannot die again; death no longer has mastery over him" (Rom. 6:9). He has an endless postexistence, just as he had an eternal preexistence.

Yes, Jesus really is God, *but* he is equally truly human. Once again, Paul encapsulates the thought: "In Christ all the fullness of the Deity lives in bodily form" (Col. 2:9). Although Christ did not preexist as a human being, in his postexistence he has a glorified human form. As the exalted God-man, he is the sole mediator between God and human beings (1 Tim. 2:5), granting forgiveness to anyone who appeals to him for salvation and becomes his follower, for "everyone who calls on the name of the Lord will be saved" (Rom. 10:13).

Appendix

A Suggested Harmonization of the Resurrection Narratives

1. After the actual resurrection had taken place, but before dawn, an earthquake occurred, an angel rolled away the stone from the entrance of the tomb, and the guards trembled and fled (Matt. 28:2–4).
2. As Sunday morning was dawning, Mary Magdalene, Mary the mother of James and Joses, and Salome approached the tomb, intending to anoint Jesus with the perfumed oil brought by other women who evidently set out later (see #7). To their amazement they found the stone rolled away (Matt. 28:1; Mark 16:1–4; John 20:1).
3. One or more of the women entered the tomb and announced that the body was not there (an inference from John 20:2, where Mary Magdalene does not simply say, "The stone has been taken away").
4. Mary Magdalene immediately returned to tell Peter and John that the body had been removed (John 20:2).
5. Mary (the mother of James and Joses) and Salome saw an angel (= "a young man" in Mark) inside the tomb

who announced the resurrection and directed the women to tell the disciples that Jesus would meet them in Galilee (Matt. 28:5–7; Mark 16:5–7).

6. These two women returned to the city without greeting anyone on the way, for their holy awe rendered them temporarily speechless (Matt. 28:8; Mark 16:8).

7. Certain women from Galilee, along with Joanna (cf. Luke 8:3), arrived at the tomb, carrying perfumed oil to anoint the body of Jesus. They met two "men" (= "angels"; cf. Luke 24:4, 23) and then returned to report the angels' message of the resurrection "to the Eleven and to all the rest" (Luke 24:1–9, 22–23) who had evidently now gathered together (cf. Matt. 26:56).

8. Meanwhile, informed by Mary Magdalene, Peter and John (and others?; Luke 24:24) ran to the tomb (without meeting Mary and Salome), observed the grave-clothes, and returned home (John 20:3–10; and Luke 24:12, if this is the correct textual reading).

9. Mary Magdalene followed Peter and John to the tomb, saw two angels inside, and then met Jesus (John 20:11–17; cf. Mark 16:9).

10. Mary Magdalene returned to inform the disciples that Jesus had risen (John 20:18; cf. Mark 16:10–11).

11. Mary (the mother of James and Joses) and Salome met Jesus and were directed to tell his brethren to go to Galilee (Matt. 28:9–10).

12. The disciples had now had reports concerning the empty tomb or the resurrection from three sources (viz., Mary Magdalene, Joanna and the women from Galilee, Mary [and Salome]), but they refused to believe these reports (Luke 24:10–11; cf. Mark 16:11).

13. During the afternoon Jesus appeared to two disciples on the way to Emmaus. They then returned to Jerusalem to report the appearance to the Eleven and others (Luke 24:13–35; cf. Mark 16:12–13).
14. Jesus appeared to Peter (Luke 24:34; 1 Cor. 15:5).
15. That evening Jesus appeared to the Eleven and others (Luke 24:33), Thomas being absent (Luke 24:36–43; John 20:19–23; 1 Cor. 15:5; cf. Mark 16:14).
16. One week later Jesus appeared to the Eleven, Thomas being present (John 20:26–29).
17. Seven disciples had an encounter with Jesus by the Sea of Tiberias in Galilee (John 21:1–22).
18. The Eleven met Jesus on a mountain in Galilee (Matt. 28:16–20; cf. Mark 16:15–18).
19. Jesus appeared to more than five hundred people (Luke 24:44–49; 1 Cor. 15:6).
20. He appeared to James (1 Cor. 15:7).
21. Immediately before his ascension, Jesus appeared to the Eleven near Bethany (Luke 24:50–52; Acts 1:6–11; 1 Cor. 15:7; cf. Mark 16:19–20).

Notes

Chapter 1: Did Jesus Exist?

1. This information is drawn from a report entitled "It Happens in the Best Circles," *Time*, 23 Sept. 1991, 59.

2. For further details on the content of this chapter, see my article "References to Jesus in Early Classical Authors," in *Gospel Perspectives*, vol. 5: *The Jesus Tradition outside the Gospels*, ed. D. Wenham (Sheffield: JSOT, 1985), 343–68. A thorough treatment of the evidence for the historicity of Jesus would require that we evaluate the authenticity and significance of the references to Jesus in the *Jewish Antiquities* of Josephus, the Slavonic version of Josephus's *Jewish War*, the Talmud, Moslem tradition, the apostolic fathers, the apocryphal gospels, heretical writings, the *Acta Pilati*, the letter of Mara bar Serapion to his son Serapion, and the apocryphal letters of Pilate to the emperor Tiberius and of Lentulus to the Roman Senate. Many of these texts are available in the collection of J. B. Aufhauser, *Antike Jesus-Zeugnisse* (Bonn: Marcus & Weber, 1913). Then, of course, there is the testimony of the New Testament documents themselves. A Jewish scholar, D. Flusser of the Hebrew University in Jerusalem, has remarked that "the historicity of Jesus is proved by the very nature of the records in the New Testament, especially the four Gospels" ("Jesus," in *Encyclopaedia Judaica*, ed. C. Roth [Jerusalem: Keter, 1971], 10:10). In addition to this documentary evidence from non-Christian and Christian sources that is relevant to any consideration of the historicity of Jesus, there is "institutional" evidence and certain psychological considerations that support his existence. The very existence and persistence of the Christian church point in this direction, for the church's "papers of

incorporation" (the New Testament) are based on the existence of its founder, and nineteen centuries of church history can scarcely be founded on a myth. Then there is the psychological improbability (1) that any group of first-century Jews, to whom crucifixion was anathema (Deut. 21:23), would invent a religion whose founder was crucified by their Roman overlords on a charge of political agitation and sedition and (2) that these same Jews would then die for what they knew to be a gigantic hoax, a lie that they themselves had created.

3. There is no certain knowledge about the nationality of Thallus. See the article reviewing the data by H. A. Rigg Jr., "Thallus: The Samaritan?" *Harvard Theological Review* 34 (1941): 111–19.

4. This fragment was preserved by the Byzantine historian Georgius Syncellus. See F. Jacoby, *Die Fragmente der griechischen Historiker II B* (Berlin: Weidmann, 1929), 1157, #256.

5. This date is advocated by R. Eisler, Ἰησοῦς Βασιλεὺς οὐ Βασιλεύσας (Heidelberg: Winter, 1930), 2:141, 435; idem, *The Messiah Jesus and John the Baptist*, trans. A. H. Krappe (London: Methuen, 1931), 298; M. Goguel, *The Life of Jesus*, trans. O. Wyon (London: Allen & Unwin, 1933), 93; F. F. Bruce, *Jesus and Christian Origins outside the New Testament* (Grand Rapids: Eerdmans, 1974), 30.

6. G. A. Wells, *Did Jesus Exist?* (London: Pemberton, 1975), 13.

7. The authenticity of this letter is beyond doubt. See the discussions of J. B. Lightfoot, *The Apostolic Fathers* (London: Macmillan, 1885), 2/1:54–56; E. C. Babut, "Remarques sur les deux lettres de Pline et de Trajan relatives aux chrétiens de Bithynie," *Revue d'Histoire et de Littérature Religieuses* 1910: 289–307; K. Linck, *De Antiquissimis Veterum quae ad Iesum Nazarenum Spectant Testimoniis* (Giessen: Töpelmann, 1913), 32–60, esp. the careful linguistic analysis on pp. 43–45; A. N. Sherwin-White, *The Letters of Pliny* (Oxford: Clarendon, 1966), 691–92, who lists the stylistic touches characteristic of Pliny, and asks (p. 691), "Where could a forger have learned about the special edict against *collegia* (private associations)?" mentioned in 96:7. Both the style and the tone are unquestionably those of Pliny—the letter is written in his inimitable florid prose and he raises questions with Trajan in his characteristically obsequious, legal tone. It might be noted that the reply of Trajan (*Epistles* 10:97) is also true to form—it strikes at the

heart of the issue with his customary terseness. As for the content of Pliny's letter, a Christian forger would be unlikely to testify to the apostasy of fellow believers and the consequent revival of pagan worship, far less to predict that a "multitude of people" would return to the state religion "if an opportunity is granted them to renounce Christianity." Nor would he have a Roman provincial governor speak so disparagingly of Christianity—as "infatuation" (*amentia*), as "depraved and excessive superstition" (*superstitio prava, immodica*), and as "this contagious superstition" (*superstitionis istius contagio*).

8. Thus P. L. Couchoud, *The Enigma of Jesus* (London: Watts, 1924), 24; G. A. Wells, *The Jesus of the Early Christians* (London: Pemberton, 1971), 185.

9. It is impossible to know the precise wording of the report given to Pliny. If the apostate Christians were accurately describing genuine Christian conviction, they may possibly have used the phrase *Christo Deo* ("to Christ who is God") (cf. the similar expressions in contemporary Christian documents: Ignatius, *To the Ephesians* 18:2; *To the Romans* 6:3; *To the Smyrnaeans* 1:1), a sentiment Pliny then expressed in the more unassuming form *Christo quasi deo* ("to Christ as if to a god"). If, on the other hand, these one-time Christians were reflecting a revised view of Christ that they presently held or if they were accommodating Christian language to pagan understanding, the phrase *Christo quasi deo* may actually have been used in the report they gave.

10. G. Bornkamm, *Jesus of Nazareth*, trans. J. M. Robinson (London: Hodder, 1960), 28.

11. Pliny says (*Epistles* 10:96:6) that these defendants "confessed themselves Christians but then denied it." Presumably they had misunderstood the nature of the charge, perhaps imagining that anyone who had ever espoused Christianity was obliged to confess to it. Pliny continues: "They meant (they said) that they had once been Christians but had given it up, some three years before, some many years previously, and a few as many as twenty years before."

12. Two problems remain in this discussion of authenticity. First, why does Tacitus refer to Pontius Pilate as "procurator" of Judea when we now know from an inscription discovered at Caesarea in 1961 that his official title was in fact "prefect"? Now it may be that Tacitus treats this term

anachronistically, either consciously or unconsciously, and uses in reference to Pilate (as he does of Gessius Florus, *Histories* 5:10) the title for an equestrian governor (viz., *procurator* = Greek *epitropos*) common in his own day. But since both Philo (*Embassy to Gaius* 38) and Josephus (*Jewish War* 2:169) use *epitropos* ("procurator") of Pilate and since Josephus refers to the governor of Judea as either *epitropos* or *eparchos* (= *praefectus*), it seems reasonable to suppose that there was a certain fluidity of terminology regarding the titles of the governor of Judea, at least in popular usage, during the period A.D. 6–66, but that from 6 to 41 the titles *prefect* or *pro-legate* predominated, while after the reconstitution of the province, from 44 to 66, the term *procurator* became the common designation. The second problem is this: It is sometimes affirmed that if Tacitus's testimony were reliable we would expect some official record of the trial and execution of Jesus of Nazareth to have been sent by the prefect of Judea to the imperial authorities in Rome. The absence of any such report casts doubt on the accuracy of Tacitus, it is said. But in fact no official records are extant that any Roman governor of Judea sent to Rome concerning any matter. Thus the absence of any report from Pilate to Tiberius is inconclusive for the question of the reliability of Tacitus.

13. R. Syme, *Tacitus* (Oxford: Clarendon, 1958), 469.

14. For example, E. Schürer, *The History of the Jewish People in the Age of Jesus Christ (175 B.C.–A.D. 135)*, rev. and ed. G. Vermes, F. Millar, and M. Goodman (Edinburgh: Clark, 1986), 3/1:77–78; H. Janne, "Impulsore Chresto," in *Annuaire de l'Institut de Philologie et d'Histoire Orientales*, vol. 2: *Mélanges Bidez* (Brussels: University Library of Bruxelles, 1934), 537–46; H. J. Cadbury, *The Book of Acts in History* (London: Black, 1955), 115–16; A. Momigliano, *Claudius the Emperor and His Achievement*, 2d ed. (Cambridge: Heffer, 1961), 32–33; F. F. Bruce, *New Testament History* (London: Nelson, 1969), 281.

15. The word *Chrestus* is the Latin transliteration of the Greek adjective *chrēstos*, which could be applied to a propitious god, a kind person, an upright citizen, a brave warrior, or a useful slave; see H. G. Liddell, R. Scott, and H. S. Jones, *A Greek-English Lexicon* (Oxford: Clarendon, 1968), 1741–42. Whereas for Greeks, *Christos* was a strange-sounding name drawn from medical or building terminology and meaning

"anointed" or "plastered," the Latin word *Chrestus* (= Greek *Chrēstos*) was a common personal name, particularly apt for slaves ("useful one"). In his *Apology* (1:4), written about 152, the Greek Christian Justin Martyr has a sustained play on the words *Christos* and *chrēstos*: "We are accused of being Christians (*Christianoi*), yet to hate what is excellent (*chrēstos*) is unjust."

16. For example, the original hand of the Greek New Testament manuscript Sinaiticus has the spelling *Chrēstianos* in the three New Testament uses of the term *Christian* (Acts 11:26; 26:28; 1 Pet. 4:16). And behind this frequent misspelling was a common mispronunciation. Writing about 197, the Latin Christian Tertullian observes that *Christianus* is derived from the word for "anointing," but when it is mispronounced as "Chrestian" (*Chrestianus*) it is derived from "sweetness" or "kindness." He concludes: "So in innocent men you hate even the innocent name" (*Apology* 3:5). It is therefore reasonable to conclude that *Chrestus* in Suetonius is simply a spelling variant for *Christus*.

17. Lactantius, *Divine Institutes* 4:7:5, written about 311. Given the testimony of Tertullian cited above (n. 16) and the widespread occurrence of itacism (the interchange of "i" and "e") in the second century, we may fairly assume that what was true early in the fourth century was also true early in the second when Suetonius was writing, namely, that Jesus was frequently called *Chrestus*.

18. For example, Acts 13:32–39, 50; 14:1–6, 19; 17:1–8; 18:5, 12–16.

19. See the discussion of Bruce, *New Testament History*, 279–83, 286.

20. Ibid., 281.

21. Goguel, *Life of Jesus*, 98–99.

22. Josephus, *Jewish War* 2:75.

23. See T. R. Glover, *The Jesus of History* (London: SCM, 1927), 7; E. M. Blaiklock, *Who Was Jesus?* (Chicago: Moody, 1974), 11–17.

24. See A. N. Sherwin-White, *Roman Society and Roman Law in the New Testament* (Oxford: Clarendon, 1963), 187–88.

25. Compare 1 Cor. 15:14: "If Christ has not been raised, our preaching is useless and so is your faith."

Chapter 2: Did Jesus Rise from the Dead?

1. With regard to the proper order of speaking in a debate, the leader of the negative team should sum up for his side immediately after the third member of the team has spoken. But because I wanted to cast the proposition of the debate in a negative form ("that Jesus Christ did *not* rise from the dead") yet also wanted the final speaker in the debate to speak in favor of the historicity of the resurrection, I have altered normal procedure and had the leader of the negative team be the final speaker. It should be noted that the names given to the six participants in the debate are purely fictitious.

2. J. D. M. Derrett, *The Anastasis: The Resurrection of Jesus as an Historical Event* (Shipston-on-Stour, Warwickshire: Drinkwater, 1982), 1–2, 38–45, 71, 85–86, 130–32 (the quotations are from pp. 2 and 71).

3. K. Lake, *The Historical Evidence for the Resurrection of Jesus* (New York: Putnam, 1907), 251–52.

4. See, e.g., Matt. 27:50, 57–66; Acts 13:28–29; 1 Cor. 15:3–4; 1 Pet. 3:18.

5. This suggestion is made by some on the basis of John 19:31 and Acts 13:29. See, e.g., H. Grass, *Ostergeschehen und Osterberichte* (Göttingen: Vandenhoeck & Ruprecht, 1956), 176–77, 179–80.

6. This saying is attributed to A. M. Fairbairn (1838–1912), the Scottish Congregational theologian.

7. This eloquent summary of Renan's view is drawn from J. M. Shaw, *The Resurrection of Christ* (Edinburgh: Clark, 1920), 165–66.

8. Keim's view is summarized by Shaw, *Resurrection of Christ*, 168.

9. W. Marxsen, *The Resurrection of Jesus of Nazareth*, trans. M. Kohl (London: SCM, 1970), 156.

10. This translation is taken from E. Hennecke, *New Testament Apocrypha*, ed. W. Schneemelcher, trans. and ed. R. M. Wilson (London: SCM, 1963), 1:185–86.

11. See, e.g., the efforts of H. Latham, *The Risen Master* (Cambridge: Bell, 1917), 225–29 (and the explanatory notes thereon, 229–41); G. D. Yarnold, *Risen Indeed* (London: Oxford University Press, 1959), 7–8, 44–47, 81–82, 121–23, 126–27; J. Lilly, "Alleged Discrepancies in the Gospel Accounts of the Resurrection," *Catholic Biblical Quarterly* 2 (1940): 98–111; J. Wenham, *Easter Enigma: Do the Resurrection Stories Contradict*

One Another? (Exeter: Paternoster, 1984); and M. J. Harris, *From Grave to Glory: Resurrection in the New Testament* (Grand Rapids: Zondervan, 1990), 160–63, which is reproduced in the appendix below.

12. See M. Grant, *Nero, Emperor in Revolt* (New York: American Heritage, 1970), 152.

13. See Rom. 14:9; 1 Cor. 6:14; Eph. 1:20; Phil. 3:21; 1 Pet. 1:3; 3:22.

14. It is probable that Mark's Gospel originally ended at 16:8; see my discussion of this issue in *Raised Immortal: Resurrection and Immortality in the New Testament* (Grand Rapids: Eerdmans, 1985), 14–16.

15. See the discussion in L. Swidler, *Women in Judaism* (Metuchen, N.J.: Scarecrow, 1976), 115–16.

16. K. E. Stevenson and G. R. Habermas, *Verdict on the Shroud: Evidence for the Death and Resurrection of Jesus Christ* (Ann Arbor, Mich.: Servant, 1981), 111–29, 155–59, 176–79.

17. G. R. Habermas, "The Shroud of Turin and Its Significance for Biblical Studies," *Journal of the Evangelical Theological Society* 24 (1981): 47–54.

18. Ibid., 54.

19. I. Wilson, *The Shroud of Turin* (Garden City, N.Y.: Doubleday, 1978), 211.

20. G. Ashe, "What Sort of Picture?" *Sindon* 1966: 15–19, cited (without specific page number) by J. Nickell, *Inquest on the Shroud of Turin* (Buffalo: Prometheus, 1983), 86.

21. The information in the next three paragraphs is drawn from an article entitled "Debunking the Shroud of Turin," *Time*, 24 Oct. 1988, 81.

22. K. E. Stevenson and G. R. Habermas, *The Shroud and the Controversy* (Nashville: Nelson, 1990), 134–47.

23. F. Cumont, "Un rescrit impérial sur la violation de sépulture," *Revue Historique* 163 (1930): 241–66. Regarding this inscription A. Garzetti comments: "Its authenticity is now universally admitted, its provenance from Nazareth is accepted, it is agreed that it dates somewhere in the period from Augustus to Claudius and should probably be assigned to the reign of the latter" (*From Tiberius to the Antonines: A History of the Roman Empire A.D. 14–192*, trans. J. R. Foster [London: Methuen, 1974], 604). For bibliography on the inscription, see pp. 604–5.

24. This is the translation of F. F. Bruce, *New Testament History* (Garden City, N.Y.: Doubleday, 1971), 301, who discusses the inscription on pp. 301–3.

25. See chap. 1 on Suetonius.
26. C. F. D. Moule, *The Phenomenon of the New Testament* (London: SCM, 1967), 13.
27. T. R. Glover, *The Jesus of History* (London: SCM, 1927), 188–89.

Chapter 3: Is Jesus God?

1. For a detailed discussion of the various strands of the New Testament witness to Christ's deity, see V. Taylor, *The Person of Christ in New Testament Teaching* (London: Macmillan, 1958); and, more recently, R. L. Reymond, *Jesus, Divine Messiah* (Phillipsburg, N.J.: Presbyterian & Reformed, 1990).
2. With regard to Jesus' life on earth, we may say either that these attributes were usually inoperative, although not forfeited, or that he possessed them in concentrated potency rather than pure actuality (to use Aristotelian categories).
3. J. R. W. Stott, *The Authentic Jesus* (London: Marshall, Morgan & Scott, 1985), 34.
4. For example, Eph. 3:14–19; Phil. 1:3–6; Col. 1:9–12.
5. John 12:44; 14:1; Acts 16:34; Rom. 4:3, 5, 17, 24; Gal. 3:6; 1 Thess. 1:8; Titus 3:8; Heb. 6:1; 1 Pet. 1:21.
6. Rom. 1:7; 2 Cor. 1:2; Gal. 1:3; Eph. 1:2; Phil. 1:2; 1 Thess. 1:1; 2 Thess. 1:2; Philem. 3; similarly in 1 Tim. 1:2; 2 Tim. 1:2; Titus 1:4.
7. Luke 2:14; Rom. 11:36; 2 Cor. 11:31; Gal. 1:5; Eph. 3:21; Phil. 4:20; 1 Tim. 1:17; 1 Pet. 5:11; Jude 24–25; Rev. 5:13; 7:12.
8. Rom. 16:27a; 1 Pet. 4:11; Jude 25.
9. For passages that emphasize the instantaneous nature of Jesus' healing miracles, see Matt. 8:13; 17:18; John 4:52–53.
10. This miracle is also recorded in Matt. 9:18–19, 23–26; Luke 8:40–42, 49–56.
11. For a defense of the historical reliability of these three episodes, see my book *From Grave to Glory: Resurrection in the New Testament* (Grand Rapids: Zondervan, 1990), 84–85, 87–88, 89–90.
12. "Jehovah" is a hybrid English word, first attested early in the twelfth century A.D. and formed by attaching (with the necessary modification) the vowels of the Hebrew word *Adonai* ("Lord") to the four Hebrew consonants y-h-w-h, giving *Yehowah* or Jehovah in English.

13. H. R. Mackintosh, *The Doctrine of the Person of Jesus Christ*, 2d ed. (Edinburgh: Clark, 1913), 419.

14. Similarly, when Jesus declared "I and the Father are one" (John 10:30), he was not claiming that he and his Father were personally identical, for John uses the neuter for "one" (*hen*), not the masculine (*heis*). Nor is Jesus simply affirming a unity of will or purpose or action between him and his Father, so what the Father wishes, he also wishes and performs. In the context Jesus has just declared that no person will be able to snatch his sheep out of his hand (10:28) or out of his Father's hand (10:29). Such equality of divine power points to unity of divine essence: "I and the Father are one."

15. See V. Taylor, *The Names of Jesus* (London: Macmillan, 1953); and L. Sabourin, *The Names and Titles of Jesus* (New York: Macmillan, 1967). A distinction should be drawn between names and titles. A *name* (i.e., a proper noun) is an identifying appellation that belongs only to one individual or a restricted number of individuals, whereas a *title* is a descriptive appellation that is based on nature, character, function, status, or attainment and is potentially applicable to any number of individuals. For instance, in the sentence "Yahweh is my shepherd" (Ps. 23:1, Jerusalem Bible), "Yahweh" is a name and "shepherd" is a title.

16. The other passages where it is possible that Jesus is called "God" are Acts 20:28; Heb. 1:9; 1 John 5:20. The twenty-two New Testament verses or passages where it has been thought that the title *theos* is applied to Jesus are discussed in detail in my book *Jesus as God: The New Testament Use of Theos in Reference to Jesus* (Grand Rapids: Baker, 1992).

17. H. R. Minn, *The Golden Prologue* (Melbourne: Bacon, n.d.), 17.

18. There is a sense in which Thomas's confession forms the climax and end of the Fourth Gospel, for it is followed by the author's statement of purpose (John 20:30–31) and chapter 21 stands as an Epilogue that balances the Prologue (John 1:1–18).

19. On no fewer than thirty-three occasions Paul directly links the terms *theos* ("God") and *patēr* ("Father") to form a single compound appellative.

20. I say "virtually," because there are the seven uses of *theos* in the singular as a generic title referring to Jesus (see §III above), two figurative uses (2 Cor. 4:4; Phil. 3:19), and several references to a particular god (Acts

7:43) or goddess (Acts 19:37) or to a divine being worthy of worship (Acts 12:22; 17:23; 28:6; 1 Cor. 8:4; 2 Thess. 2:4).

21. Matt. 27:46 = Mark 15:34; John 20:17; Rev. 3:2, 12 (four times).

22. "The use of *God* as a proper name has throughout the literary period of English been the predominant one" (*The Compact Edition of the Oxford English Dictionary* [New York: Oxford University Press, 1971], 1:1168).